MW00911314

Finding Hope

Finding Hope

Stories by Teenagers 3

**Edited by
Carl Koch**

**Saint Mary's Press
Christian Brothers Publications
Winona, Minnesota**

Genuine recycled paper with 10% post-consumer waste.
Printed with soy-based ink.

Stacey Larson, cover artist, Mercy High School, Omaha, NE

The publishing team included Carl Koch, series editor; Vicki Tyler Wilt,
development editor; Laurie A. Berg, manuscript editor; Amy Schlumpf
Manion, production editor and typesetter; Maurine R. Twait, art director; Cindy Ramm, graphic designer; pre-press, printing, and binding by
the graphics division of Saint Mary's Press.

Brooke Adams
Chaminade-Julienne
High School
Dayton, Ohio

Contents

Carl Koch
Editor

Preface

"Once upon a time . . ."

"Did you hear about the time . . . ?"

These phrases immediately attract our attention because human beings love listening to and telling stories. Storytelling is as natural as breathing, and as ancient as the cave dwellers' bragging and miming about the kill of the day around a campfire. We tell stories about the most serious events in our life, and the most wacky. We love stories for a lot of reasons:

Stories tell us who we are. When we tell other people a story, we reveal a lot about who we are—not only to them, but to ourselves. The poet Robert Frost says this about writing, "For me the initial delight is in the surprise of remembering something I didn't know I knew." In the hurry of life, we may have missed the importance of an event when it happened. Telling the story of the event helps us realize what the event really meant—even years later. So when we tell our story, we discover ourselves in new ways.

Stories help us feel less alone. As we listen to and tell stories, we realize that our story is a part of the great human story, that our feelings and experiences—while new and significant to us—are part of the universal human experience. We are not alone. Other people have felt as we do. Our story can affirm other people; their story can help us understand life better.

We encounter God in our stories. Many times when we tell stories, we begin to realize that life is filled with mystery. What we expect to happen does not happen; what does happen is unexpected. And frequently we begin to recognize the mysterious ways God has acted in our life.

We also listen to stories because they provide entertainment, because they are an outlet for our feelings and desires, and because they can make a point in an interesting way.

Stories by Teenagers

Teenagers enjoy telling their stories as much as anyone. Unfortunately, young women and men have few avenues for sharing their experiences and insights.

Saint Mary's Press has dedicated itself to sharing the Good News with young people. In the process, young people have shared their insights, courage, generosity, kindness, wisdom, patience, justice, and honesty—the Good News—with us. In 1995, we decided to invite students throughout the United States and Canada to share their stories in a more formal way.

I Know Things Now: Stories by Teenagers 1 was published in May 1996. *Friends: Stories by Teenagers 2* came out in May 1997. Both books have been enthusiastically received by teenagers, parents, teachers, and others who work with young men and women.

Student writers could withhold their name, or use their initials, their first name, or their full name. We wanted to ensure that students could be honest in telling their stories. I think that you will find the stories in this third volume to be honest and insightful, just like those in the first two volumes.

Finding Hope: Stories by Teenagers 3

Teenagers have good hearts and perceptive minds. Untold thousands of teenagers serve needy people as volunteers. They learn from and are inspired by good people, and they are the source of hope and inspiration for other people. For this volume we asked teenagers to share their stories about where they find hope and inspiration. Hope is the anchor that holds us together when life becomes hard to cope with. Hope helps us to see in the present the possibilities for a brighter future and to put our energies into creating that future.

In response to our question about where they found hope and inspiration, wonderful stories by teenagers came in from all over. After an initial sorting, I asked six students to help make the final selection: Tim Farrell, from Cotter High School; Rachel Dahdal, from Winona State University; and Tracy Klassen, Brian Maschka, Rebecca Sallee, and Matt Sticr from Saint Mary's University, all located in Winona, Minnesota. After reviewing hundreds of stories, we selected the ones in this book.

Thanks

Great thanks is due to all the students who allowed their stories to be submitted for consideration. The only unpleasant aspect of editing this book was having to omit so many excellent stories. They just could not all go into the book. We thank all of you for your contributions and understanding.

Thanks also goes to the religion and English teachers who sent in the scores of stories received. Your cooperation made the book possible.

The stories contained here are fascinating and moving. They make inspiring personal reading, will serve as excellent discussion or reflection starters, and will find a welcome spot as readings for prayer services. They might even stimulate someone to write his or her own story. Each story shows where and how teenagers find inspiration and how they hold on to hope. We feel confident that all who read these stories will be reminded of their own sources of inspiration and hope.

Elena Azul Cisneros
Red Cloud High School
Pine Ridge, South Dakota

Inspiration

Inspiration. It's sleeping in the ground. Its residence is the deep end of the pool. Only the ones who can hold their breath until they see darkness can reach it. Sometimes these travelers catch inspiration. Sometimes I do too, but only when music is playing and the sky becomes playful with dancing stars.

It's 12:40 a.m. I can't sleep. It's a weekend, and the rain slowly drizzles down in warm sheets over the land. The blinds on my window let in little lines of dim moonlight. They sleep on my carpet floor. Softly, the tears of rain tap my window.

And in the stillness of silence and whispering solitude, I hear inspiration. Its back is to my wall. It's leaning like a madman on the hard wall that shelters me. Its voice is violins, harpsichords, cellos, and trumpets. Its voice is unison and chaos. Its voice is music. My inspiration has a beautiful voice.

Through the thin blinds on my window, through the pale sheets of rain, I see the velvet cloth. I see the pearls on the cloth. It is the night sky. I see the pearls and their cosmic shine. The velvet looks soft and smoky. And I see the words, I see the colors. I see the brain that holds what I need. I see the beginning. My inspiration has a beautiful face.

Slowly I get up from my tomb. I remove my body from the crumpled sheets. Like a blind man, I feel for my pen and paper. Like a blind man, I feel for my friends to join together in mysterious union. In the night I await my beautiful inspiration.

I begin to remember. In the cool, rainy night, the mixture of music and silence, of rain and pure solitude, helps me to remember. Pictures and voices come back in a wave of memory. I remember the first time I learned what inspiration was.

I was about seven years old and living in a big city. It seemed like a storybook to me. The buildings around me were like castles, each one holding a story. I used to sit on a corner with my grandfather. We would watch people walk by and wonder what kept them going.

And then my grandfather asked me a question that would remain with me forever: "Where does your inspiration come from?"

I looked at him, but I didn't know what to say. I didn't know what inspiration was. That was the day he told me what his inspiration was. Inspiration was a huge puzzle to me. He helped me to learn the puzzle.

"I remember when I was young," my grandfather began. "I was walking through the village, and I was bored. Everything around me I knew already. I was searching for a new view."

"I was walking by a small house with an open door, and through that door I heard the most beautiful sound I've ever heard: a violin. Its notes raised my mind. I began to notice the shine of a window newly cleaned. I noticed how the sun shone on gasoline."

I listened closely. "It was all triggered by that music," he said in a whisper.

As I listened it became clear to me: Music was my inspiration. "And I remember that night in the village," my grandfather said, "I looked up at the sky and saw a falling star. I thought it was a tear from God. I then felt I knew something about the heavens."

We sat there on the corner together. I went over what he had said. I knew then that this was my inspiration. To me, inspiration is the sky and music. That rainy night in my room helped me to remember when my inspiration began. It began when I was seven years old, when a conversation occurred that changed me forever—true inspiration.

The Innocence of a Secret-Service Agent

Matthew Luhks
La Salle College
High School
Wyndmoor, Pennsylvania

A long day of school can be one of the most depressing experiences: a forgotten lunch, a test not studied for, an argument with a good friend—so many things can go wrong. Some days I come home and just feel like giving up, wondering if it is really worth all the effort. I would love to get up and say to the world, "I quit!"

But just when I am beginning to doubt myself and the rest of the world, a special person usually cheers me up and inspires me to go on for another day. He is my brother Sean, and every day, without knowing it, he reaffirms my faith in the future. His innocence and naïveté are admirable qualities, and I think that everyone can benefit from his example.

I love to hear about Sean's dreams and aspirations, no matter how far-fetched they may be. Every week he approaches me with another goal, another thing to look forward to. Last week he wanted to be a secret-service agent, and he went around the house wearing dark sunglasses and speaking code words into an imaginary headset. This week it's a professional sky diver, and he is constantly diving off the sofa into an imaginary stretch of sky. Next week it could be anything—an astronaut, a magician, a football player—no limits restrain his dreams.

It is fine for a ten-year-old boy to dream and aspire, but what would we think of a sixteen-year-old boy, or even an adult, playing make-believe? We would probably call the police or dismiss that person as insane. Why? Why are we no longer permitted to dream? "You must be practical," demand your parents and teachers, and the whole world is constantly re-minding you of the limits of your potential.

Without dreams, we have nothing to live for. Everyone should try to be more like my brother. His dreams are his livelihood, and they allow him to look forward to the future. I look at him and hope that his dreams will never be taken away. But I know that they will be. All children grow up and become exposed to the harsh, cold realities of the adult world. We can tell ourselves that they are becoming more "practical," but I know that "practical" really means "dreamless." And without dreams, we have nothing to live for.

But as I see Sean leaping off the couch, I feel happy. I guess my own dreams are lived out through him. His puerile games are all that remain of my abandoned goals and aspirations. I wish I could still hold on to these dreams, but I know I cannot. I wish we all could still hold on to our dreams, but everyone grows up.

Sean will soon mature and become an adult and under-stand the impossibilities of his imagination. As I look at him, though, I can see life running through him, and I am inspired to go on trying one more day, to hold on, to dream.

Paul Tomasik
Seton Catholic High School
Chandler, Arizona

A Legacy of Hope

Throughout my life I took my mom's father for granted. I remember him as the one who always had the video camera at birthday parties; Grandma's constant companion while attending daily Mass, watching *Matlock*, or playing Scrabble each evening; the one with the corny puns at our family gatherings; and the one who rescued us time and again in a financial crisis or a home repair emergency. A lector for daily Masses at church and an active volunteer with the Saint Vincent de Paul Society, my grandfather seemed "good" and ever-present.

My grandpa died on July 27th, three months before his eightieth birthday. It was not until after his death that I began to realize what a holy man he truly was. I discovered that he had kept a spiritual journal his whole adult life, which only my grandmother knew about. These journal entries were written during an hour of meditation that he made a habit of doing every day. He had a custom-made prayer book, typed on an old Royal typewriter. Its pages were worn from daily use over so many years. These prayers he said every day, asking God to make him a devoted husband, father, and Christian. One recently typed prayer asked for God's help in loving my dad, who had acted in very unloving ways toward my mom and our family. Knowing how angry my grandpa was with my father, I realize how hard it must have been for him to write that prayer. Also, since my grandfather's death, my grandma has discovered that for several years he had donated about two hundred dollars a month to a number of different charities.

I also found out that my grandpa had studied and learned the Greek language so that he could make his own translations of the Bible and come as close as he could to the original word of God. He had carefully written programs on his obsolete Texas Instruments computer to help him with the translations. I was told that Grandpa taught himself braille so that he could serve as a volunteer for the Society of the Blind, teaching the blind and making audiotapes of books so that they could listen to them. These things he did without asking for praise and with only a few people knowing about them.

During the eulogy at his funeral, his six children, including my mom, recounted the times when he showed them unconditional love. My Uncle Chuck described my grandfather's strong reaction to my uncle's arrest in the 1960s, when he wanted to be a conscientious objector rather than be drafted to serve in the Vietnam war. Having served as an officer in World War II, my grandpa told Uncle Chuck that he disagreed with his decision, but then he hired a lawyer for Uncle Chuck and supported his decision.

As we packed the hundreds of books in my grandfather's study—ones on Teilhard de Chardin and Saint Thomas More, and his Latin books from grade school—I gained an even richer idea of my grandpa's deeply spiritual life. These discoveries made me rethink my view of my grandpa. The fact that he did all these things, which no one was even aware of while he was living, shows what a private, modest, and spiritual man he truly was.

Since my parents' divorce in 1994, my grandpa, Arthur J. Hallinan, has been the only significant adult male figure in my life. I am beginning to realize only now that his values, his spirituality, and his ministry have left me a legacy of hope and inspiration for the future.

Angel

Jenna M. Mancini
Country Day School
of the Sacred Heart
Bryn Mawr, Pennsylvania

Many times in my life I have wanted to give up. Often it would seem easier to quit than to try and then fail. But one person in my life has taught me that no matter how difficult something seems, nothing is impossible. My twelve-year-old sister, Nina, is severely disabled, but she never quits. Nina's amazing courage and strength have inspired me to push myself forward in times of trial and to never lose faith.

Nina has had many challenges throughout her life. She cannot speak or walk, and she was diagnosed with a seizure disorder. But despite these limitations, Nina continues to persevere, and her life is filled with joy. My sister has made me grateful for things that are often taken for granted. Tasks such as brushing her teeth and feeding herself, things that other people do automatically, have taken Nina years to achieve. Sometimes I am frustrated when I work with Nina on the same task for months, and even years. It would be easy to quit when the goal seems so distant. But every doubt that I've had about Nina's abilities has disappeared when I've looked at her face and seen such determination and hope in her eyes.

Nina understands very little, but at the same time, she knows so much. Nina loves every person without question. She doesn't know about evil; she can only understand love. Nina is an angel. Her soul is not tainted by the stains of sin because sin is inconceivable to her. Nina's world is full of laughter, hugs, and kisses, and it is based upon unconditional love. It's ironic how a person incapable of so many things is exactly the type of human God intended us to be.

Nina's presence in my life has affected me remarkably. When I think about all that Nina has accomplished, I am amazed. She learned to feed and groom herself when many professionals did not think that could happen. Nina has exceeded the limitations placed on her by doctors, and she has taught me valuable lessons about life in the process. Because of Nina, I cannot give up. If my sister who has so many obstacles placed before her does not give up, how can I?

Nina is my inspiration. When I feel inconsolable or lost, I can look to my sister for hope. Nina has taught me patience and compassion that I might not have known otherwise, and yet she has done it all without saying a word. Sometimes words just get in the way.

Stephanie Jacobson
Arlington Catholic
High School
Arlington, Massachusetts

Harmony

I sit on the floor in my room, listening to the radio and humming along, tapping my pencil on the cover of my geometry book to the rhythm of the music. I hate geometry. The song ends, and the deejay comes on to take callers' opinions on a story in the news about a boy who was suspended from kindergarten for bringing a toy gun to school. I reach over and slam my palm down on the power button, annoyed at the topic.

I reach over and grab my guitar from where it's resting against my bed and begin to play. I sing to myself, "Too many lies, too many cries, too many days gone by, too many lives vaporized, all for a cause we can't find." My pick hits the bottom string, and I toss my guitar aside and grab a pen in an attempt to write down the lyrics before I forget them. I can't find a piece of paper, so I just scribble on the back of an envelope that doesn't look like anything important. I mess around with chords and notes, working on a harmony and a rhythm. After awhile my hand begins to tire of playing. I put the words on my desk next to a glass of soda, in a pile with a bunch of other random scraps. I lean my guitar back against its case, and I turn the radio back on.

I find my inspiration and hope inside my songs. I find hope inside myself—a hope that all my dreams will come true, even though for now they are just dreams. I find inspiration to pursue my musical dreams every time I turn on the radio, every time I strum my guitar. I imagine what it would be like to do for the rest of my life the one thing that brings me so much joy. At times when I am playing my guitar, I find myself smiling for no apparent reason at all. It is as if the earth, the stars, and the planets are all in line. At that moment I understand my life, and an overwhelming feeling of happiness surrounds me in a flash. But that's all it is—just a flash—because no one can feel that intense level of happiness all the time, even though you may want to.

So while the radio blares in the background and the announcer reads the news in an unemotional monotone, I try not to think about all the bad news too much. I try not to think about the crime, poverty, and senseless acts of violence that occur in the world every day. I try to sing about them instead, because we as humans have the power to change the world. And if some people out there feel that they have the power to take a life, then I know I have the power to make one life great, and then maybe even be inspired to write a song about it.

L. A. A.
Father Judge High School
Philadelphia, Pennsylvania

The Best Five Weeks of My Life

We turned and went our separate ways. She passed through the automatic revolving doors to the rest of her life, and I was carried down and away by the escalator. I felt choked, and a stream of tears flowed uncontrollably as I walked to the flight gate. I attempted to shift the cumbersome weight of the fan I was carrying in order to get comfortable, but it was no use. I stepped onto the moving walkway with the cautionary female voice, and all I could do as it carried me away was impotently watch the world pass before my eyes.

Standing before a wall of Plexiglas overlooking the run-ways, I tried to regain some semblance of dignity and self-worth. Seventies' dance music blared through my headphones as I attempted to drown my sorrows with images of disco balls and polyester leisure suits.

A litany of memories and emotions cascaded through my mind to the rhythm of the bass chords. I tried in vain to re-member each day of the past five weeks. A smile spread over my face as I recalled how we met. Our time together was so wonderful. She and everyone else at Governor's School had such a profound effect on me that I was heading home an entirely different person from the one who had left. I wished that I could stay, but I had no choice.

As cliché as it sounds, my time at Governor's School was the best five weeks of my life. Before I went away, the only purpose to my existence was to score high on tests and dream of future vindication for my toils. I had no friends, no one on whom I could vent my problems or from whom I could seek advice. My life was socially empty, and I had resigned myself to the disillusionment that this was the way my life was supposed to be. However, all that changed when I went to Governor's School.

I was finally in my element. Everyone had interests, personalities, and goals similar to mine. It was such an exhilarating and uplifting feeling to know that people existed in this world who were like me and who accepted me for who I was. It felt as if I had been raised to a higher level of consciousness. I could finally feel that I fit in somewhere. I had friends.

At the same time that I was reveling in the fact that I was no longer an anomaly, I was also exploring the diversity of these people who were simultaneously similar to me and yet so different. My fellow "Govies" were the most diverse group I had ever encountered. They were of every color, creed, and culture imaginable. At first I was a little worried that I wouldn't be able to relate to these people, but I soon realized the simple truth that had evaded me for far too long: regardless of outward appearances, all people are the same beneath the surface.

In the same way that my fellow Govies changed the way that I looked at the world and my place in it, she changed the way that I viewed myself. I don't know how it happened that she changed me so much. She somehow energized me and gave me a new perspective on life—one in which I saw true happiness for the first time in many years. She made me feel important and needed as a person, not just as someone to ask for help in science class. She gave my life purpose and value.

In retrospect, it's rather ironic that I went to Governor's School intending to learn about the scientific and concrete aspects of our world, but ended up having the most transcendental and metaphysical experience of my life. I will always remember those five weeks as a turning point that awakened me to the fulfillment that life can offer and opened my eyes to the value and necessity of cultural diversity.

Patrick O'Brien
Cretin-Derham Hall
Saint Paul, Minnesota

Terry's Road

My father and I suit up for a snowmobile run down "Terry's Road," the road named after my late uncle, who enjoyed hunting in the endless pine forest that the road cuts through. In reality the road has no name to the public. It is just another logging road that cuts through the beautiful land, like a highway to the places on earth no person outside of the rural town of Warba, Minnesota, has ever seen. In the late winter, the countryside is the most beautiful scene anyone could wish to see, like the cover of a Christmas card. We head down the county road that runs in front of our little red cabin. The cabin is simply four walls and a roof, with no electricity or running water, but I would never change a thing. Zooming down a snow-covered gravel road at fifty miles an hour on a machine half the size of a small car with no roof is quite an experience, but doing it at two o'clock in the morning is pure terror. It took us a little under five minutes to make a trip that I know as an all-day walk.

When I looked at the huge snow mound the county plow had made at the beginning of the logging road, I remember thinking how glad I was that I didn't have to shovel it. The mound was taller than I was, and no cars had been down the road in at least two months. The snow was twinkling the starlight back on my face, and the whole scene was so beautiful, I forgot about the cold for a little bit. My father decided to lead the way on his more powerful machine, so he could cut a trail through the three feet of powder that lay ahead.

As we went over the six-foot berm and crashed into the untouched powder on the other side, I was in a state of mind I wish I could bring back on command. I was nearing the end of my eighth-grade year, and I had no worries except what to do next. As we headed on, I couldn't see into the woods on either side of me or behind me, so I just concentrated on the driving. If you have ever snowmobiled, you know that the vibration of the machine can make you almost daydream while on long trips. Well, I was practically asleep when I remembered that my father was ahead of me, and that I could rear-end him if he stopped. We were only traveling at about fifteen miles an hour by then, but I didn't want to have to explain the daydream. Then we entered a really familiar area. I like to call it Blueberry Valley because one summer we found the mother lode of wild blue-berries there, hidden from even the wild black bears that frequented the other berry bushes.

Around this time I started to daydream again, and I was overlooking the valley below. The stars were reflecting off the snow, the trees were white with snow, the air was cold and brisk, and for a while I don't even remember breathing or driving or thinking; I don't even recall the roar of the engine. All I do remember is a sudden stillness and extreme peace like I have never felt before. I remember breathing the cold northern air into my body and being in total harmony with life. I had no worries, no questions, no thoughts. I felt warm inside and loved all around. Although the drive past the valley lasted no more than a minute, I felt like the world had stopped.

You may be able to recall other times like this, and so can I, but this one seemed more powerful than all the others I have experienced, read about, or been told about. At that time I felt closer to God and to my Uncle Terry than I have ever felt before. Whenever I think of that time, I know that my uncle was there in spirit with God, and that all my dreams had come true. In my mind, heaven is right there on Terry's Road. I can't explain what it feels like to be able to visit heaven whenever you want to, but I can say that I don't fear death at all, because I will spend eternity with Terry in Blueberry Valley.

(Patrick's Uncle Terry died in the Vietnam war.)

Rory Murphy
Mount Saint Joseph
Academy
Flourtown, Pennsylvania

On the Job

"203622176, Enter, Start Work, Enter," I repeat to myself as I clock in for another fun-filled day of work.

"Good morning, Rory, how was the party?" I hear a voice from behind me ask. I know, without even turning around, that it is Paulie. I can tell by the New York accent.

"Great, why weren't you there?" I ask.

"I'll tell you at break. I don't want to be late," he answers.

Paulie, my coworker, comes from the Bronx. He wears designer jeans and seven chains around his neck. He spikes his short black hair. When I first met him, I thought he looked kind of dumb. It wasn't until I actually talked with him that I found him to be quite the opposite. He works three jobs in order to pay for community college. He listens to classical music and aspires to be a pianist. He is musically brilliant—at least I think so—and I love listening to him play.

I go to the front, open my register, and begin my work as a supermarket cashier. "Why did you wear these shoes?" I question myself. I just got to work and already I'm complaining. I look over at Bill and can't help but feel ashamed. Bill is an eighty-five-year-old man with the same job as I have, but he has about ten times the energy and vibrance. Each time I glance over at him and see the smile that accompanies his service, I can't help but smile myself; his happiness is contagious. I throw on a grin, take a deep breath, and go back to checking.

At break I sit down with Tony, one of my closest male friends. We met through a mutual acquaintance, and we just clicked. I have spent practically every day of my summers with him since then. Tony is quite the character. He has the type of personality that is impossible not to love, but he also has one major problem: a strong affinity for trouble. He cannot seem to steer clear of it for too long. It always seems to be waiting out there for him. He has spent some time in jail for his behavior, but in the past year he has changed a great deal. He has finished rehab and is now a recovering alcoholic and proud of it.

Being so close with Tony over the years has taught me a great deal. He has helped me to come to the realization that anything can be accomplished with determination, and that the strength of one person's will is truly unconquerable. We talk until his shift resumes, and he promises to come over after work. I watch him as he exits into the produce section, and soon I see Paulie strutting in to talk with me.

"Hey ya, cutie, do ya wanna hear the story now?" he asks.

"Of course," I answer. He tells me some wacky tale about how this new girl he is seeing kept him "preoccupied." I know that it is simply a fabrication. He was probably too tired after running from work here to his job at 7-Eleven. I just laugh it off as I always do, while trying to drink as much coffee as possible to ensure that I will remain awake for the next three hours.

After break I finish my shift and punch out. I leave exhausted, but in some way I am refreshed. It isn't until I am walking home and reflecting on my day that I realize how immensely these three individuals have affected me. Each one has taught me a different lesson about life, but all the lessons have something in common: they all have inspired me. From them I have received a new sense of hope for the future.

In Bill I have discovered the beauty that lies in having a lust for living. The simple gesture of smiling really changes a person's attitude, and if by that small action I can make one person happy, think what I could do if I wore a permanent grin. I have discovered how easy it is to accept people for who they are, and I have a renewed sense of confidence in people, because if one person can surrender their prejudices, ten can, and if ten can, I do not see why ten thousand cannot.

Paulie has given me the inspiration to dream even the most impossible dream, because dreams are our reason for living.

Tony has given me a renewed sense of hope in our generation. We are not all sex-crazed, drug-addicted juvenile delinquents, and even those who are can change, and perhaps that is the most important thing.

As I walk home, my mind races with thoughts and emotions. I take off my shoes as I continue my journey. Despite my fatigue I look forward to tomorrow with uncontrollable zeal and to the many lessons I have yet to learn from the employees of the Sea Isle City ACME.

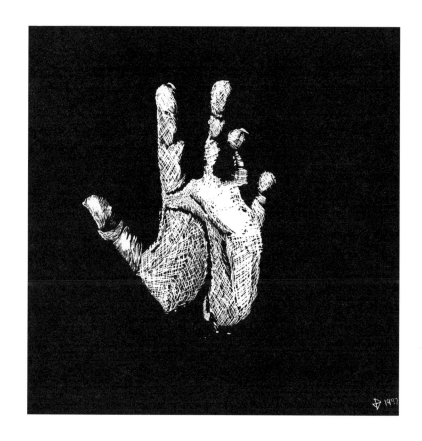

Jon Bashioum
Bishop Denis J. O'Connel
High School
Arlington, Virginia

Emily Bennett
Saint Mary's Academy
Portland, Oregon

A Double Rainbow

When I was in seventh grade, I was obsessed with being popular and outgoing. Keeping my reputation as the wildest dresser in school was a top priority. I spent hours planning my next outfit move in the game of junior-high fashion styles. One day, I remember, I wore a pleated white tennis skirt, short and cute, with a cotton, frilly poet's shirt; a faded army jacket with yellow stars on the collar; humongous, clunky shoes; and green-and-white-striped knee socks. I was crazy. Junior high was a confusing time in my life, with my melodramatic emotions changing as frequently as the tides.

In February of that year, my father introduced me to Monty Billings, a person who would change my outlook on life. Monty was the director of a camp named The Prairie Trek Expedition. My father had gone on "The Trek" when he was a kid. He clung to fond memories of excavating Indian ruins and rampaging around the desert, digging for fossils and other treasures.

I listened curiously as Monty told about a summer program where youth from all over the world traveled in big vans and saw the wonders of Anasazi ruins and desert scenery. I was thoroughly interested in finding new space. I decided at that moment that I would go on The Trek, no question in my mind.

On 23 June I stepped onto a plane headed for Albuquerque, New Mexico. I was overflowing with enthusiasm to learn about plants, animals, history, and archaeology. When I returned home, nothing was more important to me than going back to New Mexico the next summer. After a long junior-high winter, the plants began to bloom again; my plans to return to Prairie Trek were finally completed.

I think of that summer as a time when I began to dance to the music of my soul. I have thousands of clear, bright memories to cherish always. I climbed Mount Hesperus, a 13,000-foot peak that towers above the lush Colorado wilderness. I rafted the San Juan River, a body of water that held me warm and smooth. I even went on a horseback pack trip into the White Mountains of southern New Mexico; there I met my beloved mule, Chunk. But these events don't seem to add the same color to my heart as did one special day, the day we camped at Three Turkey Ruin.

Our campsite was at the edge of Canyon de Chelly. In the middle of nowhere, we made our makeshift home of Baker tents and our cozy army truck named Bessie. The ground was a soft red and brown powdery earth that sat only an inch above a hard rock layer. Sage and juniper trees were the only scraggly living plants sprinkled across the land. The perfume of desert dirt is dry and crisp; I could always catch a bit of sage wafting through the air. Our goal was to reach Three Turkey Ruin deep in the canyon below. The sun soared in the sky and baked the earth. The shelter of a passing cloud was not to be found. The blue of the sky was pure and entrancing. Its color never ceased, but spread from horizon to horizon like a shield over the earth. The night before, we had formed a dream circle and chattered until the moon set. My eyes felt heavy and my limbs slow in the morning. After only a few minutes of trail travel, though, I was feeling springy again; I merely needed the feel of the trail beneath my toes to arouse my energies once again.

The narrow and dusty path traversed the top of the canyon. From our vantage point, we could see the carved snake of a canyon meander across the land. The rock was a mosaic of different shades of brick red, burnt orange, and rich brown. The swallows swooped across the canyon and back, playing games and laughing together. After a quick mile, the trail began to slope downward into the valley of a stream bed that had dried up long ago. We crept down the steep terrain, and when we reached the canyon floor, we threw down our packs heavily and dragged out our water bottles with a sigh. Water is precious in the desert, and we appreciated every sip of cool wetness. "Hydrate or die" was our motto, and we lived by it. Hiking through the canyon, we discovered petroglyphs, ancient rock carvings chipped by the Anasazi Indians. The drawings were covered by desert varnish, a weathered brown shade that told us that these were truly the writings of someone who had lived long ago.

Marching further on, we came to our destination, Three Turkey Ruin. The Anasazi ruins were made from adobe bricks baked by the sun to last. Three Turkey was in the corner of a rock overhang, and the wall that faced us was flat with two crude windows and a key-shaped doorway. It almost groaned with old age; the weather of the canyon was slowly eating it away. The most spectacular sights were the three turkeys painted bright white on the front of this house. They watched us as we munched on our delicacy of smashed, warm peanut butter and jelly sandwiches. I gazed at those three turkeys and wondered what their eyes had beheld thousands of years earlier.

To return to camp became our next goal. When we reached the top, though, we were startled by a new sight. Dark gray, grimacing clouds loomed on the horizon. I saw that they were drenching the land in the distance from the mist and haze that clung to the ground. In moments, it seemed, the storm pounced on us. I felt a shock slither down my spine as thunder shook me and lightning ran like a knife through the sky. Chaotically we scrambled to make sure our home was waterproof. I boated my tent and made sure my mess of clothing was not going to be drenched. I threw on my stylish, shiny blue rain gear and a neon green hat, and I ran to assist others in the struggle with our disarray of belongings. We dragged extra tarps under the truck, along with tents and poles. The book box and the science box were hastily stashed in the back of the vans. I could smell the lightning; the scent was almost imperceptible, but it was there.

At that moment I was only aware of the need to get every-thing to safety. When water falls from the sky in Arizona, it does not hold one in anticipation. There is no sprinkling in-volved, only sheets of water plummeting to earth with a mission to soak. Once everyone was situated, we met in the back of

Bessie with guitars and crackers. Such luxuries cheer up any gray situation. We were laughing and singing "Waltzing with Bears" within minutes. Then came a cry from outside, "Come quick, everyone!"

Everyone fell back out of the truck, eager to witness the excitement. The clouds broke for a moment, and a bridge from heaven was revealed for us. Every bright color appeared in the droplets before us; row upon row of color contrasted with the grayness of the sky. A perfect arch was formed. Only in my dreams had I imagined such a sight. I stared, and my heart jumped because a second rainbow was appearing. It matched the first in strength and beauty but was backward—the colors went from lavender to red. A double rainbow lay before my eyes! I was sure I could reach out and catch its secrets, the truth of the world, and all the answers. My eyes filled with salty tears, and my heart pounded with the glory of nature. The rainbow slowly faded, and I turned to retreat to shelter.

A pang of loss like a sudden shadow fell over my soul with the disappearance of the colors. Yet my eyes glimpsed another unearthly sight. The clouds loosened their grasp in the sky, and sunset was nearing. Each cloud, suspended like a feather, reflected the peach and lemon rays of the sun. Layers of soft clouds hovered above the horizon. The rest of the sky was gray with rain clouds, but for a moment the sky decided to flash its wildness for me. I may have been a wild child, but I could never reach beyond the wild beauty of nature.

These memories have been in my heart since the day I left, and I know that I will not let them slip off the edge of my cluttered mind. When I returned home, I realized that I had gained a new sense of life. All my friends' social problems seemed insignificant and immature. I began to wear simple jeans and cotton shirts to school every day. I knew that part of me was still in New Mexico, seeing that rainbow and knowing the grandness of dirt and sun and sky and rock and me. In the scheme of things, I am tiny. Yet I feel full, and I have found something that I love, something I will keep seeking until the day I die; I have discovered the spark and the wild personality of nature.

Veronika Sweeny
Stella Maris High School
Rockaway Park, New York

Choosing to Raise His Daughter

Writing about a source of inspiration and hope for the future is a simple task for me. The greatest inspirational force in my life is my father. From the time when I can first remember up until right now, I have always had a deep respect for my father. He is a highly intelligent man who has achieved many great things in his life. He has earned five degrees, is fluent in Swahili, and is a successful litigation lawyer. However, it is not these worldly accomplishments that give me inspiration. I realize the value of my father's academic and professional achievements, but I am impressed more by his simple faith and his charitable heart than I am by his ability to absorb knowledge or his brilliance in the courtroom.

When my father was a much younger man, he had dreams of becoming a politician and making changes for the better in the government. He was a recent law school graduate and an avid student of political science and philosophy. Inspired by John F. Kennedy, my father believed that he had the ability to make the world a better place by becoming part of the political machine. However, my mother, a PhD in epidemiology, had given birth to my oldest sister, Indira, a few months prior to my father's graduation. My parents were desperate for money because they were both students and could not hope to support a newborn baby on student loans and grants. Fortunately, my mother was able to land a good job as a teacher, leaving my father with a very difficult decision. He could pursue his dreams and leave my sister in the care of a baby-sitter, or he could stay at home and become a househusband. My father chose to raise his daughter rather than to let a stranger do it for him. Without even a second thought, he gave up his dreams of political triumph for the sake of a small child. This is one event in my father's life that has been a source of inspiration for me. I realize the many sacrifices he has made in order to raise his six children properly.

For eighteen years my father was a househusband, seven of them spent overseas in Saudi Arabia. The years in Saudi were very hard on my father, who is a deeply religious man, because he was not allowed to practice his religion. In Saudi you were not allowed to have a Christmas tree, much less to participate in Mass. However, my father, at the risk of being deported, smuggled crucifixes and rosaries into the country. He did this to keep the faith alive in his children. He taught us our prayers and made us say the rosary once a week as a family. The memory of his courage and the strength of his faith is an inspiration to me.

My father, now a hardworking lawyer, looks much older than his fifty-nine years. His face is wrinkled and his hair is white from a lifetime of hard living. He limps due to a poorly healed tear in his ankle, and he suffers from arthritis in his thumbs. But his blue eyes still twinkle, and he's always quick with a joke or a quiet word of encouragement.

In being an inspiration to me, my father is hope for the world. I have learned from his example, and I hope one day to be just as good an example for my children. My father did make this world a better place, not by being a powerful senator or congressman, but by being a loving and kind father to his six children.

It Only Takes a Spark

K

Merion Mercy Academy
Merion, Pennsylvania

Ashbel, Caroline, and Nicholas tumbled into my life on a hot June day when I was fifteen years old. As I ran to prevent a group of four-year-olds from spilling red paint all over their shirts, I nearly tripped over this trio playing quietly in the grass. As a counselor at a local day camp, I was nearly overwhelmed with responsibility on the first day of the season. The fifteen children under my care were a lot to handle, and I found myself constantly running from child to child, tying shoes, fixing shirts, and keeping them out of danger.

In the midst of this hectic atmosphere, it was surprising to see a group of preschoolers playing so calmly with one another. Caroline, Nick, and Ash sat in the middle of the playground in a small group, inspecting dandelions. I watched them, pleasantly surprised, until my attention was drawn quickly away from these kids, and I stopped thinking about this strange phenomenon of mature three-year-olds.

Later, a small argument broke out over a cupcake during lunchtime, and I walked over to where two young boys were having a heated discussion. As I came up to them, I noticed another boy standing in the middle, negotiating.

"You don't like chocolate and this has chocolate. Now . . . wait. WAIT . . . here's Katie." Ashbel was standing between the two boys, and he seemed to have stopped their fight. They walked away happily due to their peacemaking peer, Ashbel. I asked him what had happened.

"See . . . see . . . Katie, they were fighting. And, . . . um . . ." Even though he was at a loss for words, I understood that he knew how wrong fights were and that he was intelligent enough to try to stop one. Most children that age don't have the ability to see that; Ashbel truly displayed a human characteristic that I've only witnessed in older people. I was astounded.

Over the next two weeks, I became accustomed to spending my days with preschoolers and making group bathroom trips. During one of these outings, I noticed a small figure assisting other kids with turning on the hot water.

"Caroline, what are you doing?"

"Silly, I'm holding the water on for everybody who can't reach it," she said with a giggle, as if the answer were obvious. The rest of the children never helped one another in that way. But to Caroline, taking the time to help her friends with the faucet seemed to be second nature. How many adults help one another like that?

As the camp season continued, these three children continued helping other campers who needed assistance, never getting in trouble, and keeping peace on the playground.

One day when I was particularly tired, I noticed a little set of arms wrapping themselves around my leg. Looking down, I saw Nick.

"What's up?" I asked.

"You look sad. And you need a hug. You know what? I think . . . I think that we need to hug each other a lot." And he walked away.

I was speechless. I had always known the importance of hugs, but most three-year-olds don't verbalize the universal human need for physical contact.

The days passed, and camp came to a close. I felt tears come to my eyes as I said my final farewells to Caroline, Nick, and Ashbel. These three amazing children had only been in my daily life for six weeks, but I'd remember them forever.

I have been inspired by Caroline, Nick, and Ashbel because of the acts of kindness and generosity they displayed this summer at camp. These kids showed their capacity to use human gifts—using organized thought to care for others—and gave me the hope that the world of tomorrow will be a better place. These kids haven't launched any large-scale peace campaigns, stopped a riot, ended a war, or saved a life—yet. But by their actions as preschoolers, they show an amazing potential to realize these actions in the future. I feel confident that tomorrow will be a little bit safer because of them.

The heat from a blaze can keep a world warm, but the fire must start from a single spark. I saw a spark this summer.

Cynthia G. Betlbovo
Academy of the Holy Cross
Kensington, Maryland

Katrina Villasis
Lake Michigan Catholic
High School
Saint Joseph, Michigan

Making the World a Better Place

On my second trip to the Philippines, my mother, who is a doctor, asked me to help at a free medical clinic. She would be holding it in the ghettos of metro Manila; I was not at all pleased. Unknown to me, this would become one of the most amazing experiences of my life.

The clinic was nothing more than the bottom floor of a rundown building. There were two rooms and a bathroom in the back. Each room contained a few chairs and a table. My job was to be what you could call a receptionist–nurse. I had to help the doctor, get supplies, and organize the incoming patients.

The first patient was a woman who came in coughing, sneezing, and complaining of a sore throat and a fever. Immediately I thought flu or bronchitis, but I looked at my mother, and I knew she felt that it was something more serious. She continued to question the woman, who finally revealed that she had AIDS. My mother then told the woman that she should consider going to the hospital. Hearing this, the woman refused, saying she didn't want to go. My mother pleaded, saying that the AIDS, teamed with the pneumonia, could kill her within a matter of days. Again the woman said no. There was nothing my mother could do, so she had to let the woman go, saying "Take care and God bless" as she left.

Later in the day, an old man came into the clinic. At first sight he looked fine, except for a slight limp with his right leg.

He said that all he needed was a checkup, so I sent him right in. Noticing that I had forgotten to register him, I walked into the examination room just in time to catch my mother unwrapping a wound on his foot. It was large and obviously infected. His feet were dirty. He had no shoes, just some worn flip-flop slippers. The infection had spread, infecting the rest of his leg and causing him to limp. My mother told him to go to the emergency room because his foot probably needed amputation. All that she could do was wrap it up with fresh bandages. Satisfied but saddened, the man thanked us and quietly limped through the door.

One of the last patients was a lady in her early twenties with eight children and another on the way. Obviously, they all weren't hers. They all looked to be under the age of ten. Their clothes were dirty and tight. Some of them had slippers on to protect their soiled feet. The others were barefoot. They were all so cute. It broke your heart. The lady said they all needed checkups. One by one they went in, each taking a turn and waiting patiently.

Finally it was the mother's turn, and my mom told her that one child had tonsillitis, one had a cold, and another had an ear infection. My mother gave them all the proper medication. They thanked us and left the office hand in hand, looking like a family of little ducklings.

Our day was done. We had seen about thirty patients. It was strange how before I had looked on this experience as if it were something to dread, but now I had that great feeling you get when you help someone. Nothing can compare.

This extraordinary experience has become my inspiration. I found hope for the future in my mother and people like her who sacrifice themselves and strive to help others, no matter what the circumstances. This whole ordeal has made me seriously consider a career in medicine, just like my mother. I want to be like her and the others who continually perform these selfless acts that make the world a better place.

Mariel Tatiana Fernandez
Incarnate Word
High School
San Antonio, Texas

One Little Song Opened My Eyes

For two years I spent two hours every Saturday morning at a piano keyboard, rehearsing for a concert. I had volunteered to play in an ensemble of children. Our goal was to raise money for disabled children so that they could realize their full potential through the study of music. Many of these children could not see, speak, or hear. I do not have those problems. Because my music has enhanced my sensitivities, I hoped the same would happen for them. But I still don't understand why I made such a commitment of time when I was only fourteen years old.

Five months before the concert, a little boy walked into my practice room. He sat down at my piano and played a small tune for my teacher—one he had composed. Although he was blind, he could play any song by ear. When he played that very first song at my lesson, I felt myself reaching deep inside my soul—finally understanding why I was doing what I was doing. I saw myself in him. I realized that we shared a tough outer core, he and I. His loss of sight was his protection, and it enabled him to speak from his heart. Up until that moment, my life had been robotic. Sometimes even the music that was close to my heart sounded cold and empty. After I met him, I became passionate in my music and in my life. My music opened me up and helped me to see and hear and speak.

Most teenagers my age are in a great hurry to grow up—so was I. Now I've slowed down. I take the time to look at the world changing in front of my eyes. I see the person I am becoming. Without that tough outer core, I allow those I trust to understand the real me. In turn I understand more of the nature of people, for they entrust me with their precious thoughts, feelings, and ideas. I know now that I was the one who was blind before I met this little boy who walked into my room, sat down at my piano, and played his song. I was not blind physically, but spiritually. One little song opened my eyes. That is when I understood that music opens hearts and allows the truth to be sung out loud. A little boy taught me this. He is my hope and inspiration for the future. This is my song to him:

> Searching—
> I saw him
> Led by a mother's loving hands
> His eyes innocent
> though vacant
> His ears sensitive
> to music
> His song cut through my soul
> Propelling me
> into new worlds
> with glimpses into the future
> His heart—unknown to me
> was full of understanding
> And it was there
> in his gift
> that I found God.

Jennifer Green
John F. Kennedy Catholic
High School
Warren, Ohio

The Face in the Mirror

As I stand before the mirror, I see a face reflected back that I have known and loved all my life. Her brown eyes reveal sincerity and strength, yet the sparkle is tarnished by sadness and suffering. Her complexion is flawless and pure, yet it is stained by the tears that could no longer be kept inside. Her smile is bright and welcomes all, yet it struggles to remain through the fear and anguish she encounters. I see her every day. I cannot escape the face in the mirror, but it is not mine. It is the face of my hope and inspiration, my strength and endurance: I am the only living memory of my mother. In my every action, word, and thought, I see my mother. Her spirit lives in me and acts as my source of faith as I begin each new day. A second does not pass that I do not fail to be reminded of the part of me that I have lost. As I stand before the mirror, it is my mother that I see.

As I take a look at my mother's life, I begin to wonder if I will ever be as good a person as she was. She was a woman of the utmost compassion and beauty, even when she was suffering. She had remarkable strength and courage that put me in a state of awe and wonder. Even in the hardest times of her illness, she always tried to smile before my innocent eyes. She always kept herself in touch with reality, but she never stopped dreaming.

As I remember the saying, "Always hope for the best but prepare for the worst," I find myself repeating these words of my mother's. However, I never thought about their true meaning until after her death. It seems as though she made me who I am today, knowing she was going to have to leave me. I look back and realize that I was doing things that a normal teenager would never have to do. During her illness, I felt like I was running the house—cleaning, ironing, cooking, and doing whatever needed to be done. I knew more about pills and the latest drugs and treatments than the local pharmacist. Today I look back and am thankful that I had to grow up so fast, because all my experiences have shaped me into the person I have become. I owe it all to my mother.

As I think back to the times when my mother would be waiting for me to come out of school, I am blinded by the remembrance of the first time that she was not there to greet me with her smile and embrace. I think back to the times when she helped me with those tough homework assignments, but I am saddened by the remembrance of the first time I came to a hard math problem and had no mother waiting to help me. As I see the mothers and daughters laughing as they walk through the mall together, I am overcome with a wish to walk through the mall just once more with my mother. It is funny how I have come to appreciate the little things that my mother used to do. However, it is very sad that it has taken her death for me to come to this realization. I guess we truly do not know just what we have until it is gone.

As I stand before the mirror, I wonder if I am truly making my mother proud. When I am faced with decisions, I wonder if I have decided to do what she would have done. I live for and through my mother. She is my hope and inspiration. I only wish I could share my life with her as she shared hers with me. The memories may fade, but my mother's spirit will always be alive in me and in everything I do.

M. C.
Sacred Heart School
of Montreal
Montreal, Quebec, Canada

Sweeping Away the Evil

The dirt streets were strewn with plastic juice bottles, mango peels, and disgorged sugarcane pulp. Heaps of rotting garbage lined the roadside, spilling into drainage ditches already blocked with sewage. The occasional pig could be seen scavenging on top. The numerous cement houses were floured with dust, and the atmosphere itself had an acrimonious feeling to it.

The little country of Haiti had a rough history of dictatorship under Papa Doc and his son. Using their secret police, the Tonton Macoute, they ruled with terror and corruption. The military took over for a short period, but things were just as severe. The poor people suffered, and the wealthy continued to prosper.

Finally, the time came for the little third-world country to have its first democratic election. Supervised by foreign governments, the people voted freely. The choice was Jean Bertrand Aristide, a Catholic priest long devoted to the cause of the poor. Many believed he was almost immortal, having survived more than one assassination attempt. At long last, here was someone whom they could trust to take care of them.

Aristide's political party was called Lavalasse, which in Creole means "landslide" or "sweep away." The rooster was his symbol, and it began appearing everywhere and on everything. The rooster was painted on walls, shown standing on a fallen military officer.

46

In his victory speech, Aristide said that the people had been living with "garbage" for years, and the time had come to throw it out. They had to do it for themselves. The people were inspired and took to the streets. A new feeling of hope was in the air. For three days the nation cleaned. They picked up the plastic bottles and mango peels, and swept away the disgorged sugarcane with makeshift brooms. Even old men and pregnant women worked waist-deep in refuse-filled ditches, shoveling and hauling. Children lugged stones to patch potholes in the roads.

The country came alive with vibrant color. Flags were strung back and forth across power lines. All sorts of tropical flowers were transplanted to decorate street fronts and public places. Houses were freshly painted with whitewash made from ashes. Everywhere, fantastic victory paintings appeared on walls and doorways. Suddenly the dusty towns did not seem so dusty anymore.

When the work was done, whole communities gathered to celebrate, singing and dancing into the night. It was as if a big weight had been lifted from the shoulders of the little country.

Witnessing this miraculous metamorphosis, I was changed too. Never had I seen such motivation and liveliness in these people. They had all come together to show their solidarity and support for Aristide and their new government. They believed in the future, despite the poverty and problems that still surrounded them. I could feel the energy they had created with their united spirit and effort, though I did not completely understand the politics behind it. I saw firsthand what people working together with a common goal could achieve.

Now, when I think about the serious problems in the world from my fortunate vantage point in Montreal, I don't feel that finding solutions is hopeless. I know that if there is a will, there is a way.

Francis A. Zovko
Seton Catholic
High School
Chandler, Arizona

He Died for His Country

Many things have inspired me and given me hope throughout my life, but one man has inspired me more than anyone else. Not only does this man give me hope and inspiration, he gives me a sense of pride and courage. I never met this man, but he has been one of the most significant people in my life.

It all started thirty years ago in the communist country of Yugoslavia. He was the seventh-born of nine children. He was a hardworking young man who was smart, enjoyed track, and had a promising future. It was hard for him to succeed because he was Croatian. He lived in a communist country that hated Croatians, and he feared that he would be drafted into the communist army. So, in 1970, he moved to Gothenburg, Sweden. He met his wife there, and they married in 1972. In 1974, she was pregnant with their son.

By this time the man had learned the Swedish language pretty well and was successful. In fact, he had established himself, and he was a leader to the Croatian people of Sweden. He became entangled in political affairs, and he was doing some serious work for the government. It was so important that on the cold morning of 15 December 1976, he was shot to death.

Two Serbian agents were waiting for him right outside the door. As soon as he stepped out, one agent shot him in the hand. He ran to his car and lay across the driver's seat, trying to reach for his handgun in the glove compartment. As he turned over, the two agents ran up to the car and shot him in the back numerous times. His wife and his two-year-old child witnessed this, and they ran to the car after the two men had taken off. They got to the car only to find their husband and father dead.

This brave and courageous man was my uncle. Although I never met him, he is still my inspiration. Whenever I am scared, I try to remember the courage that my uncle showed by working against the communist party of Yugoslavia. He died for his country, something that people say is the most honorable thing a person can do.

Six years ago when I went to Europe, I visited the city of Gothenburg, Sweden. I went to my uncle's gravesite and found that the letters of his tombstone were gold, and the tombstone was made of the finest marble. Fresh flowers were placed there every day. I also visited the Croatian club in Sweden. Since I was a new face there, people asked who I was. I just said I was Stijepan's nephew. At first they were shocked, and they asked if I was telling them the truth. I told them that I was, and I was immediately offered a drink, something to eat, or anything else that I wanted. My uncle was a hero, and that gives me an incredible sense of pride. My uncle gave thousands of people hope that one day Croatia would be its own independent nation, and today it is. My uncle may be dead today, but his memory and heroism will live forever. He is my hope and inspiration.

Joseph D. Crane
La Salle College High School
Wyndmoor, Pennsylvania

Cherish Life

In the world of the high school student, it is hard to find any good reason to continue to care. Our biggest dilemmas consist of having to write papers, take tests, and, on a stressful weekend, find the best party to go to. We find petty arguments to fill up our minds, we hold grudges, and we try to be "better" in all ways than everyone else. In the prime of my high school life, I was cracked between the eyes with a huge and sobering dose of reality.

One Monday I walked into school after a weekend of doing whatever I wanted. The world was so unstressful, it was almost boring. As I sat in homeroom, a friend who sat behind me called out in one of those shouting whispers, "Crane." I turned to him, expecting to hear of something meaningless that he had done since I saw him last. Instead he whispered, "Did ya hear about Nick?"

"No," I replied, with a feeling of urgency. Nick was a friend from grade school who had had brain cancer since eighth grade. "What's up, man?"

"Well, I talked to his dad yesterday, and Nick's not doing so well. He told me that this is the end, and there isn't much time left."

I couldn't believe it. This poor kid had struggled more than anyone else I ever knew. "How could it be?" I thought. If anyone ever deserved to win a battle with a disease, it was him, but now I found that while I could go on in a world without worries, my friend was in constant suffering.

I called another friend of mine after school that day and told him that we had to go see Nick the next day. He agreed, and we had a plan.

The next day came along, and I called my friend to see when we were going to leave. When I called, I found that he had gone somewhere else after school and planned to see Nick that night. We were too slow. At about four-thirty that afternoon, I got a call from my friend's little sister.

"Joe . . ."

"What's up?"

"Well, where's my brother?"

"Why?"

"Nick . . . well . . . Nick died today."

"I don't know where your brother is."

"If you see him, tell him to call me."

I had no clue what to do with myself. I left the house and walked and walked. I stopped at different places along the way to sit and think. My simple mind couldn't comprehend what was happening, and all I knew was that I had been too slow to see him one last time. I saw Nick's sister and aunt that night, and we spoke very little. His sister let loose her tears on my shoulder, and the world seemed to be still and aimless. It seemed no progress would be made for years to come. For two days I walked through life as if I weren't really there. My mind wasn't even preoccupied. It was just empty.

When the time came for the funeral "celebrations," I was a little better. It had taken me some time to find the ability to cope with a real problem. The viewing was hell. All the kids who were always so fun to be with were full of sorrow and confusion. None of us knew where to go next. It was a time for a new beginning, a time to gain an understanding of what had happened and to take this new knowledge into the life we had really just begun. I couldn't think that way then, but things were clearer after the viewing. Nick's father was strong as could be. Every kid who walked by sobbing he looked in the eye and said to them, "He is in a better place." Strength seemed to emanate from the person I would expect to be taking Nick's death the hardest.

I found then that I must live with the same strength. I was a reader at the funeral. I read, from the Book of Wisdom, a passage about God's ability to make a person perfect in a short time, and how that person would be taken from this world before they were tainted.

The whole situation left me lost, but I knew just where to go. It was strange: I found faith. For the first time, I knew that I would be rewarded if I led a good life. I don't know what made me believe it, but as I stood over the grave on that cool, sunny Friday, I felt that I finally knew something. My friend had struggled and died with a strong soul, and he now watched with God as we were all given back to the reality of the world. I left that place with a new mind-set for life. From that day on, I would try never to complain about the life I lead. I know now that no matter how bad or serious we make it out to be, our world is one with a time limit. We can't live as if time will never run out. We can't always "do it tomorrow." Most of all though, I will always cherish the times when life really is easy living.

Rebecca Bishop
Our Lady of Good Council
High School
Wheaton, Maryland

Anna C. Roberts
Convent of the Sacred
Heart High School
San Francisco, California

Dancing with Raul

As the sound of guitar and flamenco shoes beat onstage, I stood backstage ready to throw up. How was I, Anna Roberts, going to be able to do this? Why did I ever agree to dance with Raul alone? Sure, I would do fine dancing in a group of people, because I had my friends around me, but alone with Raul, anyone could see our mistakes!

The sweat began to drip down my back and face as the beat onstage slowed down. All I wanted to do was run into the bathroom and let loose all the butterflies that fluttered in my stomach. Raul smiled at me from across the stage. Why did he look so confident? Wasn't he worried that we would miss the beat or step on each other's feet? We had so many times in practice that I would not be surprised if we made mistakes onstage.

Suddenly, the girls onstage came squealing off. "Good luck, Anna!" they exclaimed. My teacher, Rosa, began to pick up the beat until it was a merry melody. Before I knew it, I was walking onstage, my hips, shoulders, and chest all moving gracefully to the beat. I held my head high and tried to look as calm as I could. I stopped in the middle of the stage and watched Raul walk out—tall, dark, and handsome.

I knew that when he reached me, I could no longer be Anna Roberts, who lived in San Francisco, went to Convent of the Sacred Heart High School, and needed to raise her grade in chemistry. No, now I needed to convince the audience that I was a beautiful young peasant girl in love with the richest boy in town. I began to tap the beat with my tall black satin high-heeled shoes as my love circled me. Suddenly we were in a world of our own. We danced together all night. I could not leave his touch; if I did, I would die of loneliness. I told him all my feelings and secrets through the expressions of my arms and face. With aggressive thrashings of his arms, he told me he loved me, but that we could never be together.

We were in love, and nothing could stop us from being together, except for morning. I was in his world, wrapped up in his arms, and I could not bear to think of morning, when it would be over. I fell into his arms when the morning came; I died because I could no longer be with him.

The lights went off and then came back on. I was still Anna Roberts who went to Convent of the Sacred Heart High School and needed to raise her grade in chemistry, but I had now overcome a huge fear of mine. I had danced in front of a crowd with Raul, and I had made no mistakes.

Flamenco dancing is an inspiration that gives me hope for the future. It is a dance that helps me to be proud of myself, my body, and my culture. It has given me a reason to hold my head higher and be proud of who I am. I can express myself and my feelings through dance in a way that I have never been able to do before. It has helped me conquer my greatest fears. Flamenco has inspired me to go out in the world and look for more opportunities and chances. It has made me comfortable with who I am and how I act. I am no longer a shy, timid girl embarrassed to speak to anyone. Now I feel I could talk to anyone and feel confident.

Flamenco dancing also gives me hope for the future be-cause I see that life is more than what is presented to me every day. I am able to understand that the world has so much more for me to go out and explore. Flamenco has lit a flame in my heart that will burn with inspiration and hope forever.

Visiting Mr. Frick

Vicki Miller
Lake Michigan Catholic
High School
Saint Joseph, Michigan

Throughout my years in high school, I've had to do Christian service work. During my sophomore year, a friend and I volunteered to visit an elderly man by the name of Mr. Frick. This was my first time visiting a patient, so I was a little nervous. In a way I regretted volunteering. I knew Mr. Frick was old and crippled, so I wasn't too sure how I would handle being with him. Having somebody with me made the experience a little easier and more comfortable.

I was nervous the whole day, thinking about how the visit would go. As we approached Mr. Frick's room, I pulled on my friend's shoulder to let her know that I was not ready to go in. For the life of me, I couldn't imagine why I was so scared. I thought maybe it was because whenever I see old people, I get very emotional. I told myself it was important that I do this, not only for Christian service, but for myself.

As we entered the room, I was overwhelmed by the stench of urine. I saw a limp figure to the right of me lying in bed, and I immediately knew that this was serious. I glanced over toward the bed, and Mr. Frick was lying there, not knowing that anyone had come in the room. A nurse from down the hall must have seen the two of us go into the room, because she immediately came to find out who we were. We told her that we were there for Christian service, and she then introduced us to Mr. Frick.

All he was wearing was an oversized diaper, and his bed-sheet only covered his feet. Half of his right leg was amputated, and he was hard of hearing. I had known Mr. Frick was crippled, but I didn't realize it was this bad. My heart ached when I saw him. It was filled with total sadness. The nurse dressed him and lifted him into the wheelchair next to his bed. The whole time he was staring at us with a look of confusion on his face. It took him a while to warm up to us, but when he did, he gave us a tour of the Whitcomb Tower as I pushed his wheelchair through the halls.

As we neared the front of the building, we heard beautiful music playing. Snacks and punch had been put out for the residents and their guests, so we decided to sit in there and talk. While we drank our punch, Mr. Frick had some cookies. He began to tell us old stories of himself and his wife. She too had stayed at the Whitcomb, until she passed away. As he got deeper into the conversation, tears started streaming down his face. My eyes filled up with tears, and for a moment I felt the sadness he was feeling.

Mr. Frick has had so many problems in his life, from losing his right leg to losing his wife. From the sound of it, he doesn't have many visitors, if any, and no support from family members. So many people put in that situation would think that things would never get better, and they'd just give up. Mr. Frick didn't.

I admire Mr. Frick for not giving up on himself, but most of all for not giving up on life. No matter how much suffering he had or how lonely he felt, a part of him always stayed positive. He has inspired me to always be positive and to have a better outlook on things. Although he might not know it, Mr. Frick has taught me that no matter what happens to you, whether it be good or bad, always look forward to another day. I am very thankful that I went to see Mr. Frick that afternoon; if I hadn't, I might not feel this way today. Mr. Frick has been a great inspiration for me and in a way that could inspire many others.

Kendall Ann Carey
Ladywood High School
Livonia, Michigan

We Can Do Anything

Although my encounters with hope and inspiration are numerous, I would like to focus on the hope and inspiration I found in getting to know a girl named Mary. I first met Mary six years ago, when I was about ten years old. Mary's parents were old college friends of my father's whom he hadn't seen in years. It was the Christmas holiday, and our home had been filled with visitors almost every day. I loved it! Having company over was one of my favorite things! I remember distinctly the day that Mary and her family were to come.

My father sat my sister, Kelly (who is a year and a half younger than me), and me down on the couch and said to us, "Girls, tonight we're having more company, so I want you to be on your best behavior. Some old friends of mine from college will be coming over with their three children. They have two sons and a daughter, Mary, who is about your age, Kendall." I was so excited—a new friend.

My father continued, "But you see, girls, there is something special about Mary. She can't walk as well as other children, and I don't want you to be surprised when you see her. She may come in using crutches or she may be carried in her father's arms."

My sister and I immediately asked why. My father answered, "Sometimes children have certain problems. There is nothing we can do to prevent some of these problems, and so children must learn to live with them. What Mary has is called polio. She can't use her legs to run around and play like you do, but in other ways she is no different than either of you. She is a very nice girl, and I'm sure you'll have a lot of fun tonight. So, when she comes over, make sure you have some games out that you can all sit down and play together, okay?"

Kelly and I were young, and we didn't care who was coming to play or if she could walk or not. A new friend's a new friend, and we were so excited to show her all the fun games we had received for Christmas.

When Mary came that night with her family, Kelly and I found out that it was true, she couldn't walk as well as we could. However, with the help of metal crutches that attached to her wrists, she did walk around our house and play all the games that we had planned. The three of us had a wonderful time that night, getting to know one another, sharing what we had gotten for Christmas, and hiding from the boys, her brothers. My father was very proud of his girls for the way they had acted, and he promised us that we would visit Mary at her house one day. That day came four years later.

It was a hot summer day, and I was now fourteen years old. My family packed up our van and headed for Dexter, where Mary and her family lived. We were off to spend the day at their house swimming, eating, attending a parade, and celebrating the Fourth of July together. We pulled up their long, winding dirt driveway at about noon. Cats greeted us as we jumped out of the van. Then out came the family from around the back of the house. We spent the whole day in Dexter. From the time we arrived to the time we left for home, smiles spread across our faces.

While in Dexter, the first thing we did was receive a tour of their one-floored, spacious home. After that, the youngest of the boys took my little sister and me out to the barn to see the kittens they had in a box there while our parents conversed, and Mary and her older brother, Matt, prepared for the parade. They were both in the high school band and would be marching in the parade.

At about one o'clock, Mary and Matt left in their car. The rest of us followed at one-thirty. The parade was spectacular!

The band was terrific, and Mary and Matt were my favorite parts. I was so touched to see Mary playing her instrument while one of her friends marched behind her, pushing her wheelchair. As she passed by, Mary's eyes were just glowing with excitement. I will never forget that moment.

When the parade was over and we were all back at the house, hot dogs and hamburgers were served. This dinner was followed by a nice swim in the family's pool. Everyone joined in the swim, playing a friendly game of shark together. I was impressed to see that Mary had no problem swimming, and she played shark just as well as the rest of us, if not better. She impressed me yet a third time when we played a game of soccer in the front yard. Mary played with her crutches and used her feet to kick the ball. She was on my team. Unfortunately, we lost to her older, stronger, and faster brother, who played soccer for their high school.

Through my experiences with Mary, I have seen that we can do anything if we put our heart into it. From watching her swim and play soccer, to watching her play in the high school band, Mary has truly inspired me. Getting to know her has been an important influence on my life. I have seen the way that she is able to remain a strong person despite the obstacle that polio has put in her path. She has overcome this obstacle, proving that with the desire to accomplish tasks, no matter how easy or difficult they may be, we can and will accomplish them if only we have hope. Mary is a great inspiration for anyone who takes the time to get to know her and who watches the way she works. She is truly an incredible person. I am thankful that I have had the chance to know her.

Jennifer Burger
Mount Carmel Academy
New Orleans, Louisiana

Derek James Brown
Billings Central Catholic
High School
Billings, Montana

The Toughest Kid in Town

"Shut the hell up, and get out of my face," screamed the young boy who, although much smaller in stature, was trying not to show any fear of the considerably larger boy standing less than a foot away. "I never said anything, and you know it!"

"I don't want to hear this," said the larger boy through his tightly clenched teeth. The larger boy turned to the side, but he kept the smaller boy in view out of the corner of his eye. He looked at the crowd that had already grown to close to fifty teenagers who were eager to witness some type of violence. "He wants me to shut the hell up, so now I'm done talkin'."

With a quick, ferocious motion, the larger boy swung for the smaller boy's face. Contact. His knuckles landed on the boy's jaw, directly below his ear. The smaller boy's neck jerked to the right, and he slumped to the ground. An explosion of cheers came from the circle of teenagers, and it was evident to every-one watching the fight that the smaller boy was out cold.

The larger boy was Brian, and I knew, just as did every other teenager in the city, that this was not his first fight. No-body could give an exact number, but there were estimates of fifty, maybe seventy-five fights, and the frightening part was that there was never any mention of him losing. And he didn't just prey on smaller kids; he was impartial when it came to confrontation. Simply put, he was feared, and it occurred to me that there was no plausible reason for his ferocious nature. He came from a loving upper-middle-class two-parent family, and according to psychological evidence, this environment usually produces stable young adults. Not Brian. Brian was short, stocky, quick, and worst of all, his acute temper often controlled all other emotions in agitated situations. He was a time bomb.

As I learned more of Brian through stories told by my friends, he became almost a living legend, a celebrity. I became fascinated with the respect and absolute trepidation he was able to inspire in the heart and mind of almost anyone who knew him, or just knew of him. His reputation and name became synonymous with brutality, and any mention of his name was almost forbidden in fear that it might get back to him. Soon, however, his love for physical combat was overshadowed by his drug and alcohol problems.

Brian would drink often—supposedly four to five times a week. This would mean weeknights, weekends, before and after school, morning and afternoon. Marijuana quickly became a habit too, and it opened doors to more dangerous drugs: cocaine, heroin, crack, and acid. Of course, this type of disregard for consequences caused Brian to begin failing in school. The hardest thing for me to accept was that this seventeen-year-old boy was no more than two years older than me, and he was involving himself in situations I had seen only on television or read about in books or the newspaper. He was untouchable.

"Derek, don't tell anyone I told you this, but did you hear about Brian last night?" Rodger looked at me with eyes that made it obvious that he would go insane if he didn't tell me the news within a few seconds.

"No, what happened?" I asked, expecting to hear another exciting story of suburban adventure.

"He got the #$@! beat out of him last night by some kid from Nevada. I guess this kid came up here to see his family, and while he was here, someone told him that Brian was the toughest kid in town, so he fought him."

I couldn't answer, mainly out of total shock and the fact that I couldn't comprehend how tough this kid would have to be to overwhelm Brian. Finally, I was able to manage a "What?"

"Brian got beat down. Can you believe that?" Rodger asked.

"No . . . I . . . are you serious?" I asked. He simply nodded his head, and I realized that he was not fooling around.

For about three months, I didn't hear of a solitary incident involving Brian. Then one Wednesday night, while I was sitting with some of my friends at youth group, I saw Brian walk through the door. Everyone in the room quit talking and turned toward Brian, and as soon as they saw him, they quickly turned around and continued talking nervously, hoping he didn't notice that anyone had been staring at him. The youth pastor went over to Brian and introduced himself, obviously not knowing who Brian actually was. He gave Brian a Bible and directed him to a chair near the rest of us. Brian sat there the entire night, not moving or speaking. He simply read his Bible. This was a regular occurrence for about a month, until I finally got up the nerve to talk to Brian.

"Hey, you're Brian, right?" I asked as carefully as I could manage. Nothing. He stared at me for about fifteen seconds before he answered.

"Yeah, what's your name, bro?" Brian asked.

I contemplated telling him a different name in fear that he might decide to throttle me later, but I chose to be brave (or just plain stupid). "Derek. I go to Central." Not only did I give him my real name but I gave him the primary location where I could be found. How could I be so dense?

"Cool. How long have you been coming to this youth group?" asked Brian in a surprisingly cheerful, curious voice.

Wow, conversation with the toughest kid in town. "'Bout a year. I really like it. Do you?" I asked, hoping that he would keep talking.

"Yeah, dude, I like it a lot, but I think a lot of these kids think that it's weird that I'm here. You're the only one who's ever talked to me."

"Really? I think it's just because they know who you are." Oh no, I'd probably offended him.

"Yeah, I think they are afraid of me, but that's why I'm here," he said, without the slightest hint of anger in his voice.

This was unbelievable; not only was I talking to the most feared teenager in town, but he seemed very receptive and interested in what I had to say. And what surprised me most was that these conversations continued every Wednesday night. But the introductory words that Brian spoke to me that first night were nothing compared to what he was planning to tell me. Nothing could have prepared me for what I was about to witness.

"Derek," Brian said in a somber voice one night, "I have changed. I talked to your youth pastor about two months ago, right after I was released from treatment. I told him about the fights, the beer, the drugs. I really spilled my guts to him. He taught me about God, about Jesus Christ. We sat down, and he read me some verses in the Bible." I saw tears forming in his eyes. "He showed me that I was a sinner and that my actions were not pleasing to God. I got angry because I knew that I had problems, and I was sick of hearing about it. But before I got too angry, he showed me that Jesus died for me, and regardless of what I had done, as long as I trusted in God and God alone, then I would join God in heaven when I died. Then he asked if I wanted to give my life to Christ, so I said yes. Since that day I have not gotten into one fight, because I realized that I have nothing to prove, and fighting does not give glory to God."

I was astounded by what I had just heard. How could this hate-filled young man be completely transformed? Then I realized that this is what it was all about. Brian wasn't interested in protecting his reputation, because his hope lay in something much greater: the assurance that in spite of his horrendous past actions, he still could be loved by God. I understood that the only hope for the future of a world corrupted by every de-testable evil was hope in eternity with a perfect God, through the death and Resurrection of our Lord Jesus Christ.

There is therefore now no condemnation for those who are in Christ Jesus. (Romans 8:1)

Kathy Cunniffe
Merion Mercy Academy
Merion, Pennsylvania

Remembering Patience

Have you ever seen Patience? I saw her many times, walking through the halls, sitting at her desk, helping students with homework. I have even spoken to her. In fact, she taught me science in the seventh grade. Her name was Sister Eileen, and she was the most peaceful person I have ever met.

Sister Eileen maintained order in her classroom by maintaining peace. If in any other class the students were rowdy while a teacher left the room, that teacher would surely return yelling and distributing the dreaded Discipline Notices. When Sister Eileen left the room one day and we became loud, her calm reaction shocked us. After all, we had been expecting our much-deserved punishment. This, however, was not the way of Patience.

She walked into the room without any lecture about what we should have been doing while she was out of the room. She simply went to the blackboard and drew a circle with two eyes, a nose, and a sad expression. Immediately there was silence in the room. No teacher could have found a better way to express disappointment to her seventh-grade students. From that day on, Sister Eileen had a friend in each of us.

One day a few of us received notes from a girl with whom we were friends. Mary had been going through a rough time. Her mother and her grandmother had died when she was younger, and she had just broken up with her first boyfriend.

All her friends received a note from her on this particular day. Mine looked like this:

> Dear Kathy,
>
> I am just writing to say good-bye. I'm going into eternal life tonight to be with my mom and grandmom. There is no point in living if I can't have Jim.
>
> Mary

We were a bunch of seventh-grade girls whose friend wanted to commit suicide. We were scared and confused, and we had no idea what to do. Though some of us tried reasoning with Mary, it could not be done. We needed someone who could get through to her, someone who would understand and would not get frustrated. That night we called Patience.

Without a minute's delay, Sister Eileen was on the phone with Mary's father. When he walked into her bedroom that night, Mary had a handful of pills, ready to swallow.

No one saw Mary for a while. She went to rehab, and then she came back, grateful that she had been stopped before she took her life. Sister Eileen often called her on the phone at night, willing to listen patiently to any of Mary's concerns.

Everyone loved Sister Eileen's class. From the instant we walked through the door, the peacefulness that permeated the room settled upon us and put us at ease. On the windowsill was her little stuffed lamb to remind her students of Jesus' words, "Come follow me." I saw her as God's messenger of peace, patience, and love.

One day when we walked into class, we found Sister waiting for us in the back of the room. She gathered all of us into a huddle and said, as if it were the most important thing in the world, "I just want you all to know, you're number one." When she turned away, I could have sworn I saw a tear in her eye. I didn't understand it then, but I think I do now.

A month later we again found her anxiously waiting for us to take our seats. When everyone was settled, she looked at each of us and said, "I have a sad story for you today." She hadn't been teaching the year before she came to our school, she told us; she'd been getting cancer treatment. By the next summer, she'd gotten well enough to teach again, and that was when she had come to us. However, she had recently found out that the cancer had come back. I have often thought that that was the day when she first brought us into a huddle in the back of the room.

She would have to leave us, she said, but she was going to come back as soon as she recovered, hopefully in time to teach us eighth-grade science. At the end of class, each student hugged her before leaving the room. I had promised myself that I would not cry, but when I saw her strong face and fell into her gentle embrace, I lost it. Funny how she was the one who was dying, yet she was comforting us. Such was the way of Patience.

Sister Eileen never did come back. After two years of sickness, she passed on to a place where I think she'll fit in much better. I often think of her when I am frustrated with life. The most peaceful, content woman I have ever known had only one secret to happiness: patience. She taught me to not just practice patience, but to be Patience.

Kate Flanagan
Saratoga Central Catholic
High School
Saratoga Springs, New York

A Test of Faith

Faith is a simple word, but it is sometimes difficult to understand. It is always with us, hiding during the better times, but showing up strong during the difficult times, carrying us through. It is not a gift—something that can be given—but a relationship with God, with our family, and with our friends, something that can grow and change but can never be taken away. Faith is a trust.

Faith is scoffed at by nonbelievers when we turn to it in times of need. They say that it isn't God who carried us and guided us through. It was ourselves only. The faith placed in God was only our own self-confidence. But when those nonbelievers face their own times of disaster, with their own world shattering and exploding around them, they too turn to faith. Faith gives us the strength to go on. It gives us the feeling of comfort, the feeling that someone else is there with us even when it seems as if we are very alone.

During Christmas 1996, my faith was tested as it had never been before. My older brother, David, got into a very severe car accident on the ninth of December. I had been sound asleep when I heard knocking at our door at midnight. I looked outside and saw a police car in our driveway. I thought nothing of this, because it was a fairly common occurrence at our house (my father is a police officer), so I went back to sleep. I was only asleep for a few minutes when my mother came into my room and told me that Dave had been in a car accident, and she was going to the hospital with my father. I waited in the living room, wide awake, for two and a half hours, waiting for someone to call and tell me that Dave was safe.

It didn't happen. My parents came home at 6:30 a.m. and told my sister and me to sit down. My father, usually calm, stoic, and unemotional, told us the truth: Dave was very seriously injured and was in a coma. The doctors weren't sure of the extent of his brain injuries or his chances for survival. It was the first time in my entire life that I had seen my father cry, as he explained to my sister and me, in his professional police voice, that he wasn't sure if his son, my big brother, was going to live.

That day was one of the most difficult of my life. I had to leave school because I was so upset. Everything had happened so fast that it seemed like the world was spinning around me. I knew that I had to be the strong one in the family. That seemed to be my role all my life, and I understood and accepted that.

When I saw David that afternoon, I couldn't believe what I was seeing. He was lying on his bed, looking tiny and defenseless, hooked up to huge machines with tubes attached to every part of his body, including a giant tube coming out of his head.

I can't remember ever being as scared as I was at that moment. It was then that I realized how fragile life really is.

The next few weeks were quite a learning experience for me. I learned much about myself and about my relationship with my family and with God. I learned that I didn't have to be the strong one because someone else had that covered, and it was God. He guided us through our ordeal.

I don't believe that God causes bad things to happen. Bad things just occur. But I do believe that God intervenes when these bad things happen. God acts through others—organizers of disaster relief funds, volunteers at soup kitchens or hospitals—and through the other little things that people do that otherwise go unnoticed.

I know that God was with us during those difficult weeks. God was with the man with the phone in the car right behind David on a desolate country road late at night. And God was with us when we received our best Christmas present ever, when David woke up on Christmas morning.

Our journey through life will not be easy. There are many bumps and obstacles, peaks and valleys, sharp turns and inter-sections. If our life were a smooth ride, free of pain, sorrow, disappointment, anger, and setbacks, we probably would not call on God. It is life's hardships that help our faith and our relationship with God to grow. I have a T-shirt that says, "What doesn't kill you makes you stronger." What doesn't kill me may hurt me, bring me pain, and disappoint me, but I know God will be there for me. And the more my faith in God grows, the better life will be for me because I will be stronger.

Daniel Barrett
Saint Joseph's
Collegiate Institute
Buffalo, New York

An Unexpected Guest

"Let us remember that we are in the holy presence of God."

Each of the eight class periods held daily at Saint Joseph's Collegiate Institute begins with these words, "Let us remember that we are in the holy presence of God."

Often these words present a somewhat difficult challenge for the eight hundred students enrolled in the Collegiate. Academic stress, school commitments, and the simple fact that remembering God has not, traditionally, been considered a top priority among teenagers can inhibit more careful reflection on this prayer, especially early in the morning with the notorious winter weather of Buffalo living up to its reputation. I have to admit that over the past four months, the constant repetition of the prayer and the increasing demands of schoolwork and school commitments have made its words commonplace and dull, and the simple request of the message has not remained as loud and clear as Saint John Baptist de La Salle would have liked it to be: "Let us remember that we are in the holy presence of God."

I began the third week of March frantically. Teachers were pouring on an excess of schoolwork and tests, suddenly forced by the approach of Easter vacation to realize that not much time was left in the school year to fit in the rest of their curriculum. Every class, assignment, or activity seemed rushed, for "March madness" was in full swing. By Wednesday I was miserable, concerned only with getting through the remaining days of school alive, not able to pay much attention to anything going on during the school day, and certainly not stopping eight times each day to remember that I, along with the eight hundred other students who were equally frantic, was "in the holy presence of God."

Thursday, March 20, was the first day of spring, normally a cause for celebration because the seemingly endless Buffalo winter was over. Spring began this year with little fanfare from me, for I had completely forgotten that it was approaching. I started the day in a lazy, sleepy haze, concerned only with reaching that time when I would be able to pack my bag and go home.

It was a horrible day. Nothing seemed to go right, and I didn't have the energy or patience to fix anything. Low test grades, tons of homework—all were amplified by my irritation, tiredness, and unshakable bad mood. By the time I reached biology class, I was finding problems with everything, and the slightest, most insignificant things were really starting to annoy me.

We began the class by standing. In the silence that followed for the opening class prayer, I started to review the basic facts of Mendelian genetics in my mind for the test I was about to take. During my "prayerful reflection" of test crosses and incomplete dominance, I happened to look outside. I had a great view from the window I was standing next to, and the sun was out for once. In fact, it was blaring loudly, calling attention to the smallest of actions beneath it: someone carrying cardboard out to the recycling bin, removing his winter jacket, and shielding his eyes from the glare; two kids, maybe four or five years old, playing in their front lawn; an older woman riding a bicycle with no snow to get in her way. Sun everywhere, falling on millions of lives full of millions of tasks and worries—and millions of pauses to notice the surrounding world. Today was the first day of spring, I realized.

"Let us remember that we are in the holy presence of God." Suddenly the eight-column Punnet square on my biology test did not seem to be such a formidable opponent. Nor did the term paper drafts or the pages of math homework or the hours of jazz band rehearsals that remained ahead. I was "in the holy presence of God," I remembered, even if I hadn't always realized it. By taking time out to recall that God is present in our life, even when the sun isn't so noticeably bright that it calls our attention to it, the future isn't as scary as it sometimes may seem to be. Instead, it is something to look forward to, for the future can be nothing but promising when it is spent with such a forgiving guest.

Brandy Harper
Saint Agnes Academy
Memphis, Tennessee

Jean Hee Shin
Saint Mary's Academy
Nauvoo, Illinois

Three Days with Christ

"What? What do you mean, volunteer work?"

"But we always go camping in the summer."

"Please let's just go camping. I've been looking forward to it all year."

Last summer, when we heard that our church youth group would be doing volunteer work instead of our annual summer camp, we unanimously complained in surprise and disappointment. The more we heard about the three days of service to physically and mentally disabled children, the more uneasy we felt.

However, despite our initial hesitation, every single member of our youth group decided to volunteer at the Raphael House, the home for disabled children. You can imagine the nervousness and even the hint of regret we felt as we walked into the strange house where we were to spend the next three days. I'm sure I wasn't the only one who prayed that the group assigned to me would be the most "normal" children in the house.

Room 203 had four boys. I will never forget my first impression of them, especially Hee-Sung and Simon. Hee-Sung was paralyzed from the neck down; his only means of expression was his unforgettable, frequent laugh. And there was Simon who, due to his blindness, seemed unfriendly and made me feel nervous and even scared to go near him. How little I knew him then.

76

I don't know when we all stopped being so uneasy and started making friends with the children, but even before the first day was over, my friends and I realized that it was not hard to fall in love with those unassuming, brave little children. I was delighted to see that the children easily accepted us and were ready to have fun despite their physical and mental limitations.

On the second day of our stay, we all went swimming. This must have been a very rare opportunity; the children seemed at once extremely excited and surprised at the sight of the swimming pool. While everyone else jumped into the water and started splashing and screaming in delight, I noticed that Hee-Sung had to remain in his wheelchair and could not join his friends. Even though he seemed to enjoy just watching and listening to his friends play, I was extremely sad to see his lonely figure on the edge of the swimming pool.

Sometimes, watching the children, I was overcome with melancholy. I could not help but ask, "Who are the parents that could abandon such beautiful children? Do these innocent little ones know what it means to be disabled in the eyes of society? What hardships, what heartbreaks will they have to face as they grow up?" But it wasn't long before the pure laughter and the playfulness of the children brought me out of my sad contemplations.

The three days sped by, and soon we found ourselves spending the last night together. We couldn't sleep that night. My friends and I sat around and shared our thoughts and experiences. For the first time I saw my friends, who always joked around and never said anything serious, share in earnest what they had felt and learned from this experience. It was almost as though we were discovering one another for the first time. We felt completely one in Christ.

If I say that I encountered Christ in the little abandoned children of Raphael House, it may seem too sentimental and pretentious, but I truly don't think that I have ever felt so close to God as I did in those three days. I felt convinced that if we all continued to care for others as we did in those three days, the world would be a much brighter, more hopeful place to live.

I came to the United States at the end of that summer, but I continued to feel the love of my youth group and the presence of Christ in my heart. A few months later, I received a letter from my friends. It was about how they are planning to go camping with the children of Raphael House next summer. I was deeply touched by that letter. I could almost hear the sweet laughter and feel the love of Raphael House, even though physically I was so far away from my friends.

In my mind I go over the letter I will write back to them: "My dear friends, You have no idea how happy and proud I am to hear of your upcoming camping trip. I knew you would keep your promise to go back and visit Raphael House. Please say hello to my little friends. I will always keep you all in my prayers. May the Lord go with you."

John Kenneth Filice
Cardinal Newman Catholic
Secondary School
Hamilton, Ontario, Canada

Warmth in Winter

In this hate-filled world, it's hard to find evidence of a better future for humanity. In a world where new discoveries are often perverted into instruments of death, it is a true comfort when one sees an act of kindness. In a society where the strong survive and the weak are destroyed, it is a rarity to see one person help another. However, it was just last week as I walked down the street that I witnessed such an act of compassion and genuine concern for another. I saw such an unselfish act that, despite the freezing wind chilling my body, my heart was filled with warmth.

On the road, cars sped by, and reaching skyward, massive structures of glass and steel forged sanctuaries for political decisions and business transactions. Below these giants, on the hard pavement, sat a girl no more than sixteen years old. She was bundled in tattered rags, and her scraps of clothing did nothing to keep the freezing cold from her skin. She begged passersby for change they could spare—pennies, quarters, dimes—anything she could use to buy food. But avoiding her outstretched hand and pleading eyes, designer suits and leather briefcases rushed past. They did not state a reason for not giving, no apology stating that they had no change on them at the present time—which in most cases would be a blatant lie—but rather hailed a taxi or gazed hypnotically at diamond-encrusted watches, as if they were late for an important meeting.

The young woman watched helplessly, eyes full of tears as the strangers strolled by. Her chattering teeth and blue hands showed that she was freezing, and her sunken eyes and pale skin showed that she was frail, sick, and in need of nutritional and medical care.

I walked toward her, searching in my pocket for some change, when a man dressed in similar attire to hers rounded the corner close to where she sat. He hobbled along, his weight pressing on a worn walking stick, wearing what could be found in the local trash and boasting, or rather cherishing, small trinkets that were once another's garbage. He too walked past the girl, not giving her a second glance, but then he stopped. He slowly turned, reaching into a hidden pocket from which he extracted a handful of change. Speaking inaudible words, he finally coaxed her into a coffee shop, disappearing from my sight. I followed them, reaching the large glass window just in time to see the man buy her a bowl of soup and a hot beverage. He escorted her to a table, allowed her to sit, and exchanged more words before leaving. Then he hobbled out of the shop, passed by me, smiled, and turned the corner.

I stood there in the cold, wearing my eighty-dollar shoes and my hundred-dollar coat. My stomach was full with a healthy lunch, and my wallet was glutted with money after just being paid. With my face pressed to the glass, breath fogging the window, I thought to myself that if a man who has nothing can give to another in need, there is hope for the future. It is not found in technological advancements and scientific break-throughs, but rather in the hearts of other people. If society can follow this example and learn to help, having no selfishness, our future will be a hopeful one.

Jennifer Kutsenda
Saint Lawrence Academy
Santa Clara, California

The Strength of All My Ancestors

I have found my inspiration and hope for the future through my family—from my grandparents, my mother, my aunts, and other relatives telling me of my Chinese heritage. They spin me the stories of their lives, webs of sorrow and joy, good times and bad times, to be heard, felt, and remembered in my heart. I've heard stories of my ancestors from long ago. Their tales are kept alive by word of mouth and passed on through the generations.

The Chinese blood flowing in my veins carries with it the natural-born responsibility to succeed in life. Raised in a Cantonese household since infancy, I have been surrounded on all sides by words of inspiration and encouragement. From my grandparents came the urge to explore the world, to experience all the sights, smells, sounds, and tastes around me, and to enjoy myself and learn as well. My mother brought me up to be an obedient child, to respect others, to follow rules, and, generally, to be a well-behaved person, characteristics she believed would be useful in the future. From everyone around me came the emphasis on school, to do the best I can and to never stop trying.

Upon reaching adolescence I entered that insecure stage that all preteenagers experience. I disliked who I was, and I was constantly asking myself, "Why did I have to be born half Asian, half Irish?" I was neither one nationality nor the other, and I felt like an outcast from both societies because I was of mixed race.

I didn't know where I stood in the world. Then one day my mother discovered how I felt, and she gave me one of the most important lectures of my life. She told me what it was like to be Chinese, she spoke of the history of my people, and she said that inside I was no different from any other Cantonese girl.

My heritage became even more important to me after I lost my grandparents. When they died, the members of my family began to tell me more stories about them. I found a new side of myself, a searching side longing to know who I really was. I had been going through a period in which I was questioning myself—wanting to begin a soul-searching journey and not knowing where to start.

My aunt spoke often of my grandparents and how they lived during the time when Japan invaded China. They had come to America with nothing, and they had not begged or borrowed. They started a business from scratch with nothing in their possession except their hope. By sharing my grandparents' story, my aunt has helped me to feel the necessity of keeping such a powerful hope alive. I feel the strength of all my ancestors before me. I hear their words, and I bear the hope that burned in their souls and now burns in mine. Hearing these stories filled me with pride and brought out the core of who I am, not the outer appearance molded by others, but the deepest part of me that remains untouched by society and forever sealed by history.

Mary Hermes
Newman Central Catholic
High School
Sterling, Illinois

Brad's Accident

When my brother Brad was born, he was a happy, healthy, well-adjusted child. He was my baby brother, and I adored him. Five days after his third birthday, however, disaster struck.

Brad had been spending the day at my grandparents' house. He was sitting under a large oak tree watching the painters put a new coat of paint on the house. All of a sudden, a limb broke free from the tree and fell on his head. This was nothing that could have been prevented; it was a freak accident. Ten years have passed since that day. Now Brad is thirteen years old, and I am sixteen. However, I remember the details of the entire ordeal as though it were yesterday.

Brad was in the hospital for nine months with spinal and brain injuries. He could no longer talk, walk, or even smile in response to us, his family. I remember the trips to Chicago's Children's Memorial Hospital to see him. I was overwhelmed at first, because it was such a tremendous adjustment to see so many other children with more severe injuries. My entire family had much to get used to, but soon the hospital became a second home. We celebrated birthdays and anniversaries in the waiting rooms, and we got to know some truly amazing people. That was the good that came from the bad. Naturally, along with the good, there was bad. For me, the hardest part was the fact that no longer could I see Brad smile or hear him laugh. For nine long months, he was in a coma, just lying there as though he was asleep with his eyes open.

As he made progress, although so slowly, Brad was moved from the intensive care unit to the third floor and eventually to a rehabilitation center. He was in rehab for about five months, and finally, after what seemed like forever, he was ready to come home. I wish I could say that things got back to normal, but I would be lying. Now we had nurses in our home four hours a day to care for Brad. This was probably the hardest. It was so hard to have any kind of private life. It was one of many new lifestyle changes. Our family also had to get used to people's questions. They seemed ignorant, saying things such as: "What's wrong with that little boy? Why are you pushing that big boy in a stroller?" Of course, now we realize that these individuals were simply curious, not rude. I felt that I should keep my friends away from Brad in case they had the same reaction I did when I first saw him after his injury.

Our lives have been changed forever. We have met some of the most wonderful people who have been involved in Brad's case—doctors, nurses, physical therapy friends, and special education friends to name a few. Not only has our immediate family been affected by what we tenderly refer to as "Brad's accident," but so has our entire extended family and our friends. Brad is on every grandparent's prayer list in the entire surrounding area.

Brad has made awesome improvements over these past years. He is still unable to walk or speak to us, but he responds with smiles and, if we are lucky, a true laugh! He recently had surgery to correct the curvature of his back, and he no longer wears a back brace. Our family treasures every smile we receive from Brad, and we love him so much. He has beaten the doctors' expectations more than once, and I have faith he will continue to thrive in school and impress everyone with the new and exciting things he learns every day.

I can apply so much of what I have learned from Brad to my present life and to the future I so often think about. Perseverance is everything. My parents never gave up on Brad or gave in when the doctors said there was no hope. Brad never gave up on himself or on his family being there to support him.

I can only hope that I will carry this trait throughout my life. That is to say, I hope I realize that the word *never* should always be challenged, and that with support anyone can beat the odds. Every time I get a smile from Brad, I am reminded of how precious life truly is. Brad is the inspiration in my life. He is proof that we can overcome obstacles and inspire others to do the same.

Shannon Murray
Stella Maris High School
Rockaway Park, New York

The Light Across the Hall

My hope and inspiration have come from a light. It is not just an ordinary desk light. To me this light shines forth hope and inspiration. This light is special because it belongs to my older sister, Heather.

Heather is eight years older than I am, and throughout my life she has been my role model. Currently she is in her third year at Brooklyn Law School. She is a hardworking student who earns every good grade she receives.

For me, senior year is harder than I expected and very time-consuming. I figured that taking five challenging courses in junior year would make senior year seem easier. On the contrary, the classes this year are even more challenging and require more independent work than last year. Also, playing on sports teams five or sometimes six days a week leaves less time for schoolwork. The combination of my schoolwork, sports teams, and extracurricular activities causes me to become depleted and stressed for time. The college application process is also long, so long it often seems endless. On occasion, after a long school day, a club meeting, a hard practice, and a college essay, I will open my books to do my homework, only to collapse into them moments later and begin snoring.

My bedroom is directly across from Heather's, and when I sit at my desk, I can see her room at such an angle that I only see her desk. My inspiration comes when it is late or I am tired, but I still might have one more assignment to complete. I debate whether I should skip it and go to bed or stay up and force myself to complete it. Then across the hall I see a light on. I look up and discover my sister at her desk—coffee in one hand and a pen writing furiously in the other hand. With that sight comes my inspiration to take a deep breath, open my eyes, and concentrate on my work.

This renewed inspiration from the light of hope that shines so brightly in Heather's lamp happens quite often, almost nightly. I think that if my house was dark and nobody else was up, I would either fall asleep at my desk trying, or I would give up and go to bed. However, thankfully, my role model has been able to "shed her light" on me, and in doing so, give me the inspiration to continue.

I think that God has helped shed this light of hope, because many things have happened in order for this situation to occur. First, of the six bedrooms in my house, mine and Heather's are the only two in a separate hallway, located directly opposite each other. Second, between college and law school, my sister worked for a year. Luckily, we are now graduating the same year, and had she not worked for that year, she would probably be in Australia right now, where she plans to be next year. Third, my sister was going to get an apartment near school because of the long days she spends there. Fortunately for me she was unable to find one, and she decided to live at home for her third year.

This combination of circumstances has allowed me to seek inspiration and hope as often as I glance across the hall. I thank God that I have a role model and a great sister who shines her inspiration with a radiant light of hope.

Sharon Trinidad
Saint Francis School
Honolulu, Hawaii

My Son, Nathaniel

In the weeks I spent brainstorming for this essay, I was completely stumped. I had absolutely no idea what to write about. Then one day, when I was not even thinking about a topic, I found one right under my nose. I have my son to write about. My son, Nathaniel, is the source of my hope and inspiration.

Having a baby at a young age forces any parent to take a good, hard look at the future. Personally, having a child gives me the encouragement I need to strive for the best. It gives me a reason to work hard, to be more responsible, and to be the best person I can be.

Nathaniel is a very special child. He has a condition called congenital central hypoventilation syndrome, a condition in which breathing does not occur when a person is asleep. His special needs have challenged me in many ways. Another challenge in my life is the fact that I am still a full-time student, working hard to become a successful person. I want to show my son that I can make something of myself, that I can be someone he can look up to and be proud of. My son needs to know that although he has not come from a typical family environment, he, too, can be provided for just like any other child.

Nathaniel has inspired not only me but many other people around him. My family, for example, has become a lot closer. Before he was born, we constantly bickered, our conversations were always filled with tension, and we could never work together. Now we have learned how to interact with one another without arguing, and we have civilized conversations.

Nathaniel's medical condition has also given hope and inspiration to others. He has come out courageous, defying the doctor's grim prognosis. Nathan has proven that there is hope for a child to live and function normally with his condition. He also gives inspiration to other families to continue to have faith, to know that their child can be healthy again, and to never lose hope.

In conclusion, my son, Nathaniel, has given me hope and inspiration for the future. He gives me a reason to stay in school and to never give up. His presence in my life encourages me to become a successful person so that together we can have a bright and happy future. Nathan is a constant reminder to look toward the future with hope and confidence.

Michaela Elizabeth Knipe
Saint Mary's Academy
Nauvoo, Illinois

Not Afraid of Dying

It was the summer of 1995. I was just about to turn sixteen years old, and I was ready to drive. It was then that we learned that my godfather, Joe Hopp, had cancer, and that because it had been caught so late, it would probably be terminal. I was shocked. What I heard next surprised me even more. Joe decided that he was not going to have chemotherapy or radiation treatment. He wanted his last few months of life with his friends and family to not be wasted by trying to prolong his life by a few more days. He wanted the time to be quality time.

Joe was not afraid of dying. He made that very clear to all of us by his actions and words. He knew that his fate couldn't be changed, and he accepted that his life would soon be over. He never second-guessed God, or if he did, he did it in private. He was the rock for all of us, and yet he should have been leaning on us. He was the one in pain, but he saw our pain as greater than his.

Throughout my lifetime I can always remember Joe being around, because his family and mine did just about everything together. As a little girl, I remember looking up to Uncle Joe as more of a grandfatherly figure. He gave me little treats and piggyback rides, taught me how to walk on stilts, but yet corrected me in a gentle way when I was wrong. I generally ran to him when everyone else yelled at me. He was always there to pick up the pieces.

I remember when I was about four or five years old, and we were having a picnic down along the river. I was playing in the bushes and got a thorn in my hand. I went screaming back to the group of adults, and my dad, who is not very good under pressure, was freaking out, but Joe calmly picked me up and pulled the thorn out of my hand. Then he reached in his wallet and got out a Band-Aid. He gently placed the Band-Aid on my hand, and wouldn't you know it, I was soon as good as new. That's the way I remember Joe all through my life.

Joe's birthday and mine were only one day apart, and we celebrated together for many years. He teased me, and I teased him back. He loved practical jokes, and I loved to laugh. He was compassionate, and so was I. He treated me like one of his own. He never drew any lines, and I was always considered family.

Joe never judged anyone, and he always gave you fair consideration. Even if you had done something wrong in the past, you had a fresh start with him. He was very even-tempered. He rarely yelled that I know of, except when he hit his thumb with a hammer, and he rarely ever yelled when he did that either.

Most people think of the cancer survivors as the heroes and the winners, but my family and friends are the winners for getting to know and love Joe, and Joe is the hero. He was and still is my hero.

This is dedicated to the memory of Joe Hopp and to all those who have struggled with cancer.

Tara Converse
Billings Central Catholic
High School
Billings, Montana

My Mother, My Hope

It was a warm day in Bozeman, and the campus hummed with excitement. It was commencement day, and my mom was graduating from the school of nursing. The school was having a small ceremony of its own, and my brother, grandfather, and I were there with my mom.

We sat and listened to a few speakers, and finally the president of the college began to call the names of the graduates. The graduates were allowed to bring their close family members on the stage with them, and a loved one was to pin the official nursing pin on the graduate. When Mom's name was called, I was given the honor of pinning her.

My feelings of pride and joy about my mother's graduation were present not only at that moment but every time I think of her accomplishments. Her example brings me hope for the future.

My mother graduated fourth in her high school class and had a full scholarship to Carroll College. When she enrolled in college in the fall of 1975, she couldn't have known what her immediate future would hold. My mom and dad dated in high school and went to Carroll College together. By January of the following year, my parents married due to an unexpected pregnancy. My mom was not disappointed but rather excited about having a child and starting a family. My parents dropped out of college and moved back to Billings.

After a rough few years, they bought their first home and had another child, me. We lived together for eleven years, but things between my parents were not working out. They divorced in 1990, and it was decided that my brother and I were to live with Mom.

My mom had worked as a waitress, a bookkeeper, and a secretary, but she had no professional training, and her desire to go back to college was something she had needed to squelch for years, not only for personal reasons but for financial ones as well. After the divorce, though, Mom made the decision to go back to school and pursue her dream of becoming a nurse.

The years following her decision were the hardest that my mom, my brother, and I have ever gone through. My mom worked full-time and went to classes in the evenings for the first few years. At the time, I was finishing elementary school, while my brother, Jason, was beginning high school. My mom taught us responsibility and trust, because we were expected to do our homework and chores without being asked and to do whatever was asked of us around the house. We also had to keep quiet during her study time. My mom endured so much stress during those years, and Jason and I had a hard time at first, but we realized early on that this was the way we were going to be living for a while.

After a few years, Mom had to add more classes to her load, and she began to work only part-time. With finances dwindling and time together even more scarce than money, our lives were stressful to say the least. But we trudged on together, and Mom continued to stay up all night, go to work for a few hours, go to school, and return home to housework, followed by homework. I would wake up at four o'clock in the morning and hear her typing away or see that her light was still on, and then I would see her go off to work a few hours later.

When I was in eighth grade, my mom had to go to Bozeman for a semester in order to complete her required classes. This time was especially difficult for all of us. Being away from her was agony, and the need for her to get good grades was top priority so she could stay in the program. My mom worked so hard in Bozeman and, of course, did very well.

With only one year to go, my mom began to work hands-on with patients, and her dreams seemed to be coming true. She was tired and we had little money, but Mom kept going. Finally, graduation day arrived. Mom passed her nursing boards exam and was finally done.

My mom became a registered nurse, and she was hired by Deaconess Hospital for the medical surgical floor. Today she takes care of patients going into surgery or recovering from surgery. The pride I feel when I think of what my mother has accomplished is hard to describe. She sacrificed so much. My mother struggled through financial hardship and emotional hardship, as well as physical stress, for five years. She went on without a husband and without a sturdy financial foundation and raised her children to be independent, responsible, and caring people.

What she did to overcome her tragedy inspires me more than any other great person who has lived. Her strength gives me hope. I feed off of her strength and live to follow her example. Because of what she has done, I believe that no matter what has happened in the past or what the current situation is, there is a way out; some way can be found to make things better. Even if it means sacrificing, you can still find a way to meet your goals and be successful. I believe that there will always be a way to succeed. My mother is a living example of this. She is a living, breathing example of my hope.

Amy Kling
Trinity High School
Garfield, Ohio

Katie Kalis
Divine Child High School
Dearborn, Michigan

Life Is a Roller Coaster

I, like many people, take my life for granted. I live in a world that to some people would seem absolutely perfect. To me it's routine. When I met Chris, everything I had taken for granted became the most important things in my life.

I met Chris the summer before I started high school. For a while we remained acquaintances, but nothing more. Our senior year rolled around, and one night at a party, Chris and I clicked. We became the best of friends. We both had a similar outlook on life, and we had a great time together. We would go out often. As with many best friends of the opposite sex, Chris and I began to become more than best friends. One day we announced to our friends that we were officially dating. This was of no surprise to any of our friends, but it was fun and exciting nonetheless.

That special time of year soon rolled around, that time when Cupid slings his bow and arrow, when guys and gals swoon, and the chocolate companies make a real killing—Valentine's Day. Chris and I decided to go out for dinner and a show. Dinner turned out to be a disaster. We ended up at a complete dive, but we made the best of it.

As we were sitting there, Chris looked into my eyes and said, "What do you think of life?" The question smacked me in the face. I sat there with an expression on my face that said, "Huh?"

I didn't really know what to say, so I answered with: "I don't know. What do you mean?"

Chris sat there with a very heavy look on his face. Finally he began to tell me stories about his parents and his life that absolutely horrified me. Every story he told became more and more spine-chilling.

I looked at this person that I had known for four years, and I couldn't believe how stable and how intelligent he was. It absolutely amazed me. The reason I tell this story is because Chris is an inspiration to me. Even though his family life is dysfunctional, he is happy, but more important, he is himself. His situation isn't typical, because life isn't typical. He never hides who he is, and he is an extremely well-rounded and intellectual individual. I see him as a model of someone who has had nothing, and I compare him to myself who has had everything. Life is a roller coaster; it has its ups and downs, but it is always a heart-pounding ride.

I know that many kids like Chris grow up in similar situations, but they don't always look past those terrible moments to focus on their positive qualities. Chris is one of those kids who did, and he has inspired my life as nothing has before. Chris is the hope for the future. He is an example not only to people in a similar situation but also to people like myself who have everything and take it for granted. Every one of us has a Chris inside us. By finding that strength, we can all realize that determination and inspiration are our roller coasters as we soar through life.

Traci Haddock
Arlington Catholic
High School
Arlington, Massachusetts

Hope for a Better Future: U2

When I was about six years old, I saw my first music video on MTV. (I know, I know—what does MTV have to do with hope and inspiration? Just wait and hold on for the ride, and you'll find out.) The video I saw made a strong impression on me, even though I didn't know what it was at the time. It would be years later before I realized that the wonderful video I had seen was "Where the Streets Have No Name" by U2, from their album *The Joshua Tree*. The loud music and busy scene (the band was on top of a liquor store, and hundreds of fans had shown up for the video shoot, along with dozens of police officers) had grabbed my attention in a heartbeat. I found the video so different and exciting compared to the normal dullness of "C is for Cookie," and I was drawn in.

Years later when I was in the seventh grade and just coming into the music scene, I discovered U2 in an unusual way. I was thirteen years old and starting to read odd science fiction books (okay, okay—they were comic books) that, in their own odd way, introduced me to music. Two characters in one of my comic books were getting married, and their wedding song was "One" by U2. "U2?" I asked. "Who the heck is U2?"

Determined to hear this song, I begged my mother to take me to a music store. I purchased *Achtung Baby*, the U2 album containing the song "One," and for the first three months or so, I listened only to that sad yet uplifting tune. My older sister,

98

Nicole, finally convinced me to listen to the entire album. I listened to the loud, gritty guitar and thundering drums over and over again, until I could finally hear a song within the noise.

Amazingly, I found myself rapping my fingers on the table to the songs' beats. I slowly fell in love with *Achtung Baby*, and I longed to hear more. Other albums, such as *The Unforgettable Fire*, *The Joshua Tree*, and *War*, soon caught my attention, and I quickly bought all of U2's records.

During those early teenage years, my life was turning upside down and inside out with the sudden challenges of junior high and then high school. U2 became the only constant in my life, and these four men filled me with hope. Through both song and action, they showed me how different people can be, but also how to handle those differences without the need for violence. These four wild Irish roses showed me how to accomplish things I had never thought were possible. They showed me that if four high school kids from Dublin, Ireland, could make it in the world, then a kid from rural Massachusetts had a chance, too.

This band consists of four men, two English and two Irish, although they all grew up in Ireland and are considered Irish. David "The Edge" Evans is the lead guitarist, with singer Bono on back-up guitar. Adam Clayton is the bassist of the group. Larry Mullen Jr. is their self-taught drummer. Paul "Bono" Hewson is the lead singer, with "The Edge" on back-up vocals. They formed the band in 1976, while they were still in high school, and they eventually rose to become one of the most popular bands in the world. By 1987 they had made six records, the last one being *The Joshua Tree*. With such well-known anthems as "Where the Streets Have No Name," "I Still Haven't Found What I'm Looking For," and "With or Without You," the album literally made them worldwide music stars.

With the end of the 1980s and the beginning of the 1990s, U2 decided to change their style. With the birth of *Achtung Baby* in 1991, U2 exploded again with a new tour titled ZooTV. *Achtung Baby* quickly destroyed their old image and created a new, gritty, noisy image that they gladly embraced. This sudden change in music and demeanor showed me that I shouldn't be afraid of change, since it always happens. Instead, it taught me that I should challenge the "normal" things in life and create change in myself and, hopefully, in others. By drastically changing themselves and their music, U2 gave me the inspiration to challenge ideas and form my own opinions.

The band members are very genuine (a rare thing these days) in their beliefs for peace, as shown during their concerts, a fact I find admirable. U2 has been known to actually stop a concert if "moshing" or other acts of violence are happening in the audience. They refuse to allow anyone to be injured at one of their concerts.

The way that U2 supports peaceful organizations such as Amnesty International and Greenpeace has given me a hopeful outlook on the future, knowing that many fans, including myself and my sister, join these organizations because of U2's example. Amnesty International is a worldwide organization focused on helping achieve the release of political prisoners who have been taken captive for their beliefs. Greenpeace is an association that is also concerned with human rights, as well as with keeping the environment clean and pollution-free.

One of my favorite songs from U2's twenty-one years of music making is "One." It is a melancholy yet uplifting song that tells a story of struggle and hope, of our need to help one another because we are all one, even though we are not all the same. These ideas are relevant to everyone's life, not just to a single person's existence. Bono (the lyricist for most of their songs) says what life's about and how hard it is, but he also states that "we have to carry each other" through the tough (and the good) times in order to have any hope at all for our future. We can live in this world, but we have to live in this world together if we are to accomplish any of our dreams and hopes for the future.

Over the past few years, I have learned to interpret U2's music and actions as demonstrations of peace and hope. They've given me the hope that I will succeed in my life and have the inspiration to fight for a better future, even though I've never met any of them. This goes to show that people whom you don't know personally can still affect your life greatly. All you can say is "thank you" to the open air and hope that someday they'll hear you. And maybe, just maybe, you'll finally find what it is you're looking for—happiness.

Johanna Mihok
Saint Agnes Academy
Memphis, Tennessee

Angelica Jiménez
DePaul High School
Wayne, New Jersey

Turning Back to God

I was walking into my house one day when I noticed the tears that filled my mother's eyes. I glanced across the room and saw my father's face lost somewhere within his hands. I felt as if I were in one of those dreams where you try to scream, run, or fight back, but you just can't. Finally, I was able to walk out of the room, but without saying a word. I went upstairs, where I found my two sisters talking. When I walked into the room, they stopped talking, looked up at me, smiled, and walked out. Now I knew something was wrong, and I was not supposed to know about it.

A few seconds later, I found myself listening to something I thought I would never have to hear. The way my sister hesitated to speak and the way the words came out of her mouth really scared me. All I remember from the conversation was my sister saying, "Daddy has cancer." This is what I wasn't supposed to find out about, well at least not on the night of my eighth-grade graduation. As I was sitting there in my cap and gown that night, all I could do was picture my dad all by himself at home. He had no one to yell at or to question about why it had to happen to him.

As the months went by, I could see that Dad's cancer was slowly killing him. It overpowered his body, but as it reached his soul, he fought back. For some reason I believed God was doing the fighting in his soul.

My father never talked about God, and he hadn't been to church in about ten years. Cancer is what made him turn back to God. He began reading the Bible and praying, but still he couldn't get himself to go to church. Finally the day of his big operation came. He pulled through it and through all his other operations. I really don't know what he was thinking as he was being told that his cancer was all gone. If it were my guess, I'd have to say that he was thanking God.

This is where the inspiration comes in. I saw a disease enter a cold man's body, and instead of killing him, the disease brought a new life, a life in which everything revolves around God. My father has never missed a day of church or forgotten to read his Bible at night since that day. Knowing that his life was almost taken away from him, he has become the "daddy" that this disease had taken away from us. It was amazing to see how quickly a life could change simply by letting God into it.

Jennifer Morioka
Cornelia Connelly School
Anaheim, California

Innocent Prisoners of World War II

The words kept running in my head as I struggled to keep the tears from pouring out: "I will never, in my entire life, experience the pain that my parents did. I don't know how for all those years they never even once mentioned to me about being in the camps—to hold all that pain inside and raise a family in spite of everything against them, takes more strength than I will ever have."

Those words from the daughter of the head organizer of the Tule Lake Pilgrimage (which commemorates the Japanese internment at this relocation center during World War II) left a heavy silence on the buses as people reflected on their emotions about the four-day journey. I was already lost in thought. . . .

I remember standing on the few decrepit structures that were left, imagining how these Americans must have felt. The foundations of the bathrooms and showers seemed neglected and forgotten in the vast farmland, like the people incarcerated here fifty years ago. The silence dwelling in the lava rock basin was uncomfortable, so I stood on what used to be a *fu-ro* (Japanese bathtub), raised my head to the sky, took the energy concentrated in my belly, and yelled loudly. My yell didn't make the echoing sound I had expected. It was muffled by the wind. Maybe that's how the prisoners had felt. Regardless of the protests they made, the court appeals for their constitutional rights, no one heard them. They were voided into this oblivion.

The towering mountain range encircling the campgrounds formed permanent barriers that emphasized the hopelessness of ever trying to escape. Barbed wire surrounded the camp, enclosing the Americans like cattle. It served as a reminder of how degraded their lives had become.

And yet natural balances were shifting to maintain their existence. Through the confusion and, at times, the loss of identity, love grew. There was an unspoken loyalty between the internees. When there were food shortages, due to food stealing by War Relocation Authority (WRA) employees, families would share their rations with one another. A comradery developed within their new community; everyone cooperated to make the best of what they had. Even the old photographs on display told the story of their optimism: I choose to remember the picture of a couple dancing in the gymnasium. The young man had dipped his partner, and both were caught in mid-laugh. People find things to be happy about.

Then images of my grandma pasting magazine clippings about the internment camps in her scrapbook and of my grandfather delivering an impassioned speech during a church service sprang to my mind. These images made me wish my grandparents were here to tell me their story.

As I sat on the bus headed back to the San Jose station, I could not hold back the tears. I was feeling mixed emotions. One was a feeling of sadness that the internees had had to endure so much prejudice from their own country. The other feeling was of pride for my grandparents. Their indefatigable will to survive and care for their family under such hardship inspires me. For me it was a paradox to be there, to feel not only the darkness of the event but also the light that nature, love, and families can bring even in the worst of times. Things are reborn, and there is hope.

Alisha Ruiss
Saint John's College
Brantford, Ontario, Canada

You Were Always There

In general I am a lonely person. All my life I have related best to adults, and although I get along with most people, I am not close to any of my friends at school. Usually I tend to bury this loneliness with busyness and frequent smiles to make the world believe that I am okay. Until recently I did not think that I had ever been of great importance to anyone outside my family.

It was Holy Week, and our drama class was presenting the stations of the cross in tableau for the school liturgies. In our group's scene, I was Mary grieving at the foot of the cross as Jesus died. Afterward my friend Sheila came up to me and asked if we could talk. I hardly ever saw her because she was only taking one course at school, and the rest of the time she worked. At first she didn't seem to know how to begin. Then she said that seeing me up on stage had made her feel really emotional.

"It's probably because there's so much going on in my life now," she remarked. "I'm leaving high school and my friends. I have a lot of expenses right now with my car. I'm working so many hours, and in May I'll find out if I've been accepted into college." I still didn't know where she was headed with the conversation. Then she said, "You know, when I look back over the years here and remember our play and the music trip to Nashville, I just keep seeing you. We were never really close, but you were always there."

It was true that Sheila and I had not been close, but I realized that I often called just to say hi, wish her a Merry Christmas, ask about her boyfriend, or whatever. We talked a little while longer about her hopes for college and the future. Then she had to leave for work, so I gave her a hug and promised to pray for her.

The rest of the day I pondered the words that had had such a great impact on me: "You were always there." Could a person's mere presence really make a difference? Quite often I had come up with a negative answer to that question, concluding that listening ears, smiles, and concern shown for others were taken for granted and would be quickly forgotten.

Sheila's display of gratitude restored my faith in humanity. It also made me recognize some of my own selfishness in playing the role of the lonely, self-sacrificing martyr. From now on, instead of asking, "Why, Lord?" I will try to see my troubles as an opportunity to be like Simon of Cyrene or Veronica, who, by just being there, lightened the weight of Jesus' cross.

Mary-Helena McInerney
Arlington Catholic
High School
Arlington, Massachusetts

Grampy and Nana

My main sources of hope and inspiration for the future are my grandparents. From my grandparents I have learned to be loving and strong and to treasure every moment I have. My grandmother is sick with a disease called progressive supranuclear palsy, in which her motor skills have deteriorated, and then her memory. Every day my grandfather feeds Nana, cleans her, and tries to talk with her, things that she can no longer do. Her vocal cords have failed, and now she is unable to talk, just moan and groan. It is hard to try to talk with her.

My grandparents live with us now, and whenever I go downstairs to visit them, I try to have a conversation with Nana while Grampy is either reading the paper or working on his boats. He likes to build battleships out of wood. He carves every little thing, from the guns to the boat itself. Because Nana is unable to talk, I have made up a kind of language with her. When I ask her a question, she blinks once for yes and twice for no. It is very hard to go down and visit them because every time I see Nana lying there, helpless, I want to cry. But I have to be strong, like my Grampy.

Every night before I go to bed, I sit and listen to them singing "A Bicycle Built for Two." Grampy sings the words while Nana grunts along. It is a special moment. I remember the tape I made for my mom for her birthday. On the tape Nana and Grampy are singing two songs together: "Hupa Jupa," which is a

Polish song, and "Happy Birthday." Nana could still talk and sing then.

During our school magazine drive, I asked Nana if she would like to order a magazine. She tried to say yes, but all I could hear was a noise, so I reminded her of our code: blink once for yes, twice for no. She blinked once. Then I started naming magazines she used to read when she could hold a magazine.

"Let's see, Nana," I said, "there's *McCalls* (no), *Family Circle* (no), *Redbook* (yes)." So I promised her I would order it for her so we could read it together. She made an attempt at a smile. Then I started to laugh and smile, so she tried to laugh, too.

Sometimes I sit and talk to my mom about what is going on and how Nana is doing. Nana is not getting any better. We always end the conversation with the fact that my grandparents, her parents, could die any day. No one really special to me has died yet, and I do not know what I will do when someone close to me does die. I know that when Nana dies, Grampy will die shortly after her, because he cannot live without her.

When Nana was in a nursing home, Grampy stayed with her from morning until night. He was even able to get Nana home again. He was miserable without her. At night before I lock the downstairs door, I check on them to make sure everything is okay. I look in and see Grampy sitting in the wheelchair, laying his head on Nana. Sleeping. They have been together for fifty-five years. He won't even sleep in the bedroom, because he cannot sleep two rooms away from Nana, who lives in her bed in the living room.

Every day my grandfather used to tell me, "Your nana is getting better and better, and soon she'll be walking." I would smile and agree with him. I could not bear to wreck his hopes. That was when Nana could hold herself up and walk from her wheelchair to her bed, although with a lot of help.

Sometimes I wonder how Nana must feel, knowing that she is dying but not knowing why. Every day, though, she puts on her wonderful smile and tries to laugh with us. I only wish that I could be as strong as my grandparents.

From my grandparents I have learned a lot of things: to have hope that things will get better, to be strong and face what is ahead, and to love and cherish everything that I have. I hope that when I get older, I will be like my grandparents, appreciating every day they have together. And as I go on in life, I will have the inspiration of my grandparents to help me through each day. That is why my Nana and Grampy are my hope and inspiration.

Jackie Reichert
Saint Wendelin
High School
Fostoria, Ohio

Georgina K. Vaca
Ramona Convent
Secondary School
Alhambra, California

You Can!

Trapped! That was how my mother felt when the doctor announced to her that I was in the process of developing and coming into this world. In fact, I was very unexpected. I had been the result of a passionate night with a man who had been "just a friend."

My mother had been married in Mexico City at a very young age to an individual who was a beast. He was first-class macho, and what he said or demanded, my mother was forced to comply with. This man was so vicious that when a chore was not done to his satisfaction, he would drag my mother by the hair and beat her until she was black and blue.

Time dragged on until my mother finally decided that if she did not do something about her situation, she would end up either seriously injured or possibly dead. Filled with courage and tremendous fear, my mom took the initiative to take her two kids and flee her husband and the country clandestinely.

In 1977, my mom and my beautiful brother and sister landed in South Gate, California, with only the notion that Mom would work hard to help her children and herself survive in a foreign country.

Finally my mother got settled, and while attending school to learn English, she encountered a classmate who was soon her friend, and then in 1980, he became my father. Mom's pregnancy was emotionally harsh for her because knowing that she had

112

fled from one tough situation, she had now involved herself in another.

I have definitely found inspiration in my mom because, despite the fact that she went against her cultural values and her Catholic faith by conceiving me out of marriage, she had the dignity to take responsibility for what she later called her "beautiful mistake."

"¡Tu puedes!" ("You can!") and a great big hug are my mom's favorite greetings when I come home after a hard day at school. What I appreciate most about her is that she encourages me to work toward all the goals I set; I have never heard a negative comment from her about my dreams for the future.

Yes, my mom has fears and insecurities, yet she puts them aside in order to give me her support. I find hope in the future through her history, because I believe it was not by chance that my mom conceived me. I know for a fact that God has a plan for me.

Angela M. Baumler
Lancaster Catholic
High School
Lancaster, Pennsylvania

The Meanest Teacher in School

Inspiration comes in many shapes and forms, sometimes when we least expect it. Sophomore year I began lifting weights and practicing basketball after school. As one of the only females in a predominantly male weight room, I found it hard to find a partner to do drills with and to talk to.

One day, as I was aimlessly bouncing a ball off the wall, around the corner came one of the meanest men in school, Mr. Carr. He patrolled the halls looking for someone to yell at, just waiting to give out detention slips. He rounded the corner and called my name, and right then I knew I was going to get it.

He came over to me, grabbed my ball, and began passing with me, and as we tossed around the ball, we began talking. He told me about his love for the game of basketball and about his church and family. I told him about my fear of trying out for the basketball team and how I worried about passing tests.

As someone else came around the corner, Mr. Carr quickly passed the ball back to me and yelled down the hall at some boys who were running and carrying on. He told me he'd see me the next day and to stop bouncing the ball off the wall because I was chipping the paint.

Day after day Mr. Carr, gruff on the outside and a teddy bear on the inside, made time to talk to me and to ask me how my day was going, and day after day I looked forward to having a conversation with him. The next year, though, I began to see less and less of him, until one day news spread that he was sick. I decided to do some investigating and find out just what was wrong.

When I heard the truth, I wanted to scream—cancer. He had been an avid smoker all his life, and now he had lung cancer that had already spread to his brain. It was fatal, and he would not be coming back to school again. Through the next year, Mr. Carr had radiation therapy and began to grow weaker and thinner as the disease slowly ate away at his body—but not at his spirit. He still attended our basketball games, sitting in his usual place, but this time with an oxygen tank.

One of the best feelings in the world was cutting down a piece of the net after our team won the state championship and giving it to Mr. Carr, the man who loved the game so much. My senior year he grew worse, and he fought his battle as I struggled with my own. I wanted to quit the basketball team because things were not going the way that I had planned. I wasn't getting playing time, and the team was having a bad season. But one thing changed my outlook on the situation. I looked up in the stands during overtime of the biggest game of the season, and I saw someone else sitting in Mr. Carr's seat. I knew right then that if Mr. Carr wasn't going to quit, then I wasn't going to either. As he lay in a hospital bed and struggled to stay alive, I was taking for granted my health and my youth by considering quitting basketball because of my selfishness.

Mr. Carr has passed away, and I will never forget his memory or all that he taught me. He made each day of my life that he was a part of a little brighter, and because of him I believe that one person can make a difference.

Name Withheld
Saint William of York
Parish
Baltimore, Maryland

My Secret

I know that I'm too young to understand the trials and tribulations of adulthood, but I feel I've had to grow up too fast. My parents are very supportive of my activities. They've always been right about my friends, and they've always been there to pick up the pieces after disappointments. From the outside my family may seem normal, but we have a secret.

My mother is the youngest of six children, and her oldest brother is old enough to be her father. She grew up in a strong Irish Catholic family in Baltimore. When she was growing up, most of her siblings had moved out already. There wasn't much for my grandmother to do to release her frustration, so she turned to my mom as a punching bag. Apparently this happened quite often over the years.

Maybe my grandmother was abused as a child—I'm not sure. See, my grandmother had Alzheimer's disease for many years before she died, and her childhood was not open for discussion in my house, but I suspect that she was abused. My mother sought refuge in my grandfather, who made sure she had the best Catholic education that money could buy.

It was in college that my mom met my dad. They dated and became engaged. They had to push the wedding date up a couple of months because when my mom went home for the summer, she was beaten badly.

116

In fact, the beating didn't stop until my grandmother died. I still remember a night when I was about ten years old, and my grandparents had come over for dinner for my grandfather's birthday. My mom and my grandmother had a fight that ended with my grandmother trying to beat my mother with her cane at the dinner table.

So my mom was abused by her mom. That's probably why she didn't know how to deal with her own anger. My mom has abused me, my older brother, and my younger sister all our lives. My brother remembers once when he was about two years old and my mom beat him in public. Ten years after she beat me with a belt one night, I still struggle with vivid nightmares of the infamous night, and I am still dealing with my anger about it. I've never really talked to my sister about the situation, but I know she feels the pain every time she gets cracked in the mouth. My family never discusses it. As a matter of fact, the only reason I know about my brother's experience is because my mom told me when I confronted her in the hope that something would change. It didn't.

The thing I've never been able to figure out, and probably never will, is why my father has never done anything to stop her attacks of violence. It has taken me seventeen years to realize that I'm not just angry with my mom for beating us but also with my dad for not stopping her. Yet no one dares to confront the subject, which I compare to an elephant because it's big and everyone sees it but no one dares to disturb it. Until one day . . .

I was in school, and it was almost the end of the year. My friend noticed a bruise on my face and inquired about it. My thoughts and words got all jumbled. I think that's what attracted even more attention, because most of my peers were surrounding me before I could answer. I thought I had covered it with makeup that morning, just like all the other times; I guess the heat had caused the makeup to sweat off. I think I told everyone that I fell, but those two minutes are such a blur. The truth is that my mom had hit my jaw with her keys when I talked back to her as we got into the car. I knew that I needed to talk to someone, but who?

I finally told Bob, a volunteer at my youth group. Since then he's taught me so much about myself and my situation.

Bob has helped me so much that I don't know where I'd be without him—probably dead—because he has definitely saved my life. I've come away realizing that even if I do something to provoke my mom's anger, I don't deserve to be hit, and it's not my fault that she reacts in that way. I also know that the pattern stops here. My children will never suffer the fate of my hands, the sting of being hit.

I've come so far since that first talk with Bob, a talk that has led to many other talks since then to keep me on track. And though my mom says that I deserve to be hit, I've found the courage to tell her that I don't. She can never shake that thought from my mind, no matter how she hurts me, physically or emotionally. And since the day of my first talk with Bob, some of the resentment and all of the revenge have left my mind. I'll never fight back by stooping to my mother's level, unlike what I swore I'd do when I was younger.

My relationship with Bob has grown stronger. I feel I can tell him anything. I thank God every day for sending him to me. I truly believe that God sent Bob to me for a reason. I believe him to be my guardian angel, my light at the end of a long, dark tunnel who will be with me wherever I go, even if it's only in spirit.

Standing up to my mother has made me a better person. I have more self-confidence, and I know better than to believe the labels she, or anyone else for that matter, pins on me to destroy my confidence. And I'm glad my secret's out. I've started confronting that elephant. And though there's a long road before me, there's nothing I'd do to change the road behind me. I once was weak in spirit, but with help I am growing strong. My children will thank me.

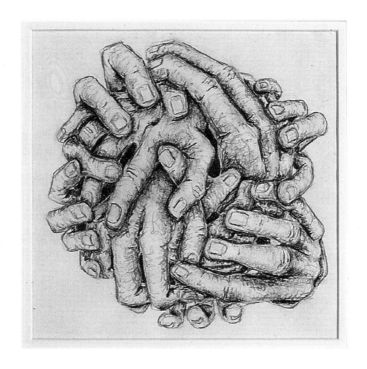

Gerri Sattele
Saint Pius X High School
Atlanta, Georgia

Maria Steinhauser
Lake Michigan Catholic
High School
Saint Joseph, Michigan

Paradise Island

Two summers ago my family, my uncle, my aunt, and my two cousins went on a canoeing trip in the Algonquin Wilderness in Ontario, Canada. It was to be eight days of canoeing and backpacking in the wilderness without any sort of civilization around us. Before we left I felt kind of leery about the whole thing. I wasn't sure if I was physically capable of the trip. We were going to canoe across large lakes and then portage across islands, carrying our own packs and canoes. There would be nine people and three canoes, three people in each canoe. The longest portage was three and one half miles. We were going to have to canoe all day for ten hours straight.

I was also the youngest and the weakest of everyone who was going. It was definitely going to be a full-body workout. I was not sure if I would be up to it mentally. We would have no showers and no great home-cooked meals. We would eat freeze-dried food. All we could bring along were one change of clothes for warm weather and one for cold weather, a tent, a sleeping bag, a small backpacking stove, food, and matches.

I remember feeling a mixture of excitement and fear when we were getting ready to shove off from the dock where we rented the canoes. I had never done any serious canoeing before in my life. By the time we canoed to the first port, I had gotten the hang of the canoeing strokes, and we had even gotten a rhythm going. I was absolutely dead by the first night. We all ate quickly (trying not to taste the food) and went straight to our tents and off to sleep.

I woke up the next morning dreading the day of canoeing ahead. By the time we got started, though, I was thoroughly enjoying it. The sun was hot and beautiful, and the water and islands were gorgeous. I was so excited when we portaged right around a huge waterfall. I could feel the cool mist dampen my skin.

When we reached our destination, it was awesome. We renamed it Paradise Island. It was so beautiful and relaxing! We swam, we talked, and we enjoyed the view and the wildlife. Loons were flying overhead, fishing in the water, and making beautiful noises.

The next day we had a huge storm. It was so cold, and of course we didn't have any shelter besides our tents, which were soaking wet. It made me realize how fragile life is. It finally stopped raining that evening. As we sat around the fire trying to dry off and warm up, I felt as if I had taken a huge breath and thought, "Hey, I pulled through it!" Then we canoed for three more days until we got back. I was so happy that I could do it.

This vacation made me realize that a person can live without material things and still enjoy life. I actually enjoyed those eight days more than most of the other days in my life when I have been at home with a shower and a bed. My trip to Paradise Island inspired me not to take material things for granted and not to make them so important in my life. It also gave me hope for this planet. This was one of the most beautiful places I have ever seen, and nobody was trying to build factories or roads on it, or trying to cut everything down for some other purpose. I saw for myself that not all the beautiful places on this earth have been destroyed.

On the Line

Pearl Carmen Hernandez
Ramona Convent
Secondary School
Alhambra, California

One day several years ago, twelve little girls suited up for yet another championship game, but this one was different. This was not the same championship game that we won every year. This was the game that no other team in our school's history had ever made it to. This game would enable us to pursue our goal of playing for the state championship.

I was a member of the sixth-grade basketball team from my grammar school, All Souls. We were a bunch of girls who had been playing together since the third grade, and it was our last year in this division. We were so excited, and so were our loyal fans, our parents. We had finally accomplished part of our goal, which was to be able to step foot on that court and say that we were one of the players that went to state. We had arrived at the game site, Bonita High School in California. As we entered the gym, I can recall feeling full of awe that we had made it this far. As we began to warm up, I could not help looking into the bleachers as they began to fill with people.

Seeing my mother and the other parents smiling brought a smile to my face, too. Once the buzzer went off, we went to our benches. As we began to pray, I remember looking into the eyes of my teammates, my friends, and seeing their nervousness, which drew more nerves inside of me. I knew at that moment that I had to become strong, because they depended on me as much as I depended on them.

After each of our names were announced, we began the game. The game went on, and the scoring continued to be close. While the fans cheered and the clock ran down, my nervousness began to fade away. Finally, with about one minute left on the clock, the score was 24 to 23, and we were ahead. My nervousness easily returned when our opponents scored another basket. This gave them the lead by one point, 25–24.

Only three seconds were left on the clock, and our coach called a time-out. As my team huddled together, my coach said: "Pass the ball to Pearl. Pearl, you drive straight to the basket and shoot the ball before the buzzer." A chill went through my spine as he looked at me and said, "You can do this, baby!"

With confidence from my coach, encouragement from my teammates, and cheering from the fans, I approached the court with a heart of full power, but the nerves of a child. With three seconds left, I got the ball, dribbled down the court, and shot as the buzzer went off. I missed the shot, but I got fouled. With no time remaining, I had two free throws to shoot.

The referees cleared the court, and my coach told me, "Pearl, you got us this far; you can do it again!" If I made one shot, we would tie. If I made both of them, we would win. If I missed both shots, we would lose.

As I approached the free throw line, the gym grew silent. No more cheers, no more talking—just complete silence. As I looked over at my teammates, I saw their little scared faces, and then I was handed the ball. Dribble, dribble, dribble, and as I stared at the rim, my eyes filled with tears. I shot the ball, and I made it!

I heard a loud cheer go through the gym as I let out a sigh of relief. I had one more shot to go in order to win the game. Once again everyone in the gym became silent, and I was handed the ball. At that moment, from the corner of my eye, I saw a boy waving his hand with the intention of distracting me. Well, it worked! It made me more nervous, but I remained strong. Dribble, dribble, dribble, and as the tears fell from my eyes, I shot the ball. I made it!

I turned to my teammates in shock as they ran to me screaming and crying. The girls tackled me on the floor, full of joy, and I felt no pain at all. Our fans filled the floor in order to congratulate us, and someone's dad picked me up to show everyone that I was the one who made the shot. Finally my team of twelve little girls had made it to the state championship.

This is a moment that I can play over and over in my head. It was a time that made me realize that I can do anything. It was one of the happiest days of my life! Having to overcome the fear of losing and letting people down is something that many people do not face and understand until they are older. I knew from that moment on that I could do anything if I tried.

My experience opened my eyes to everything that is in front of me—my future. Since this experience, I have been able to accomplish many things through the years, because I have had hope and inspiration, and I knew what it took. To make those two free throws took so much strength not only from me but also from the eleven other girls on the bench, from my coach, and from everyone who was supporting us. I have learned so much that has made me stronger and has taught me that support from others can take a person a long way.

Since that game, I have never faced anything else that has put so much pressure on me. When I do face a time that puts pressure on me again, I can look back to that important game for inspiration. Life can be very tough, but when I know that I am confident enough to handle the pressure, it makes things a whole lot easier for my mind, my heart, and my future.

Jen Toronski
Trinity High School
Garfield, Ohio

Lori Hennessy
Saint Catherine's
High School
Racine, Wisconsin

The Courage Within

My dad died on 18 September 1992. He was only fifty-eight years old, and I was only ten. In those ten short years that my dad was in my life, he taught me things that take most people a lifetime to learn. He taught me how to face life with courage and dignity, and to accept the fact that you just can't change some things in life.

It's a warm summer day, and I'm rushing home to see my dad. I'm so scared that one day I'll come home and he'll be dead. My dad has been sick since before I was even born. He has diabetes and heart problems and many other things that I can't even remember. Almost a year ago, he had a leg amputated. Right now I'm worried that he may have to lose his other leg. How will I be able to handle this? I'm so scared!

"Dad!" I yell as I rush inside.

"I'm in here, Lori. You don't have to yell."

"Dad, did the doctor call with the results?" I ask nervously. I notice the smile slowly fade from his face.

"Yes, Lori, he called. I'm afraid they have to amputate my other leg." I felt the tears start to stream down my face. How can this be happening again? I thought. How am I going to handle this?

"It isn't fair, Dad. Why does this have to happen?"

"Lori," he said, "I know that this is hard to handle, but life isn't always fair. You need to trust in God and find the courage to face your problems in life."

How could he say that? How could he just sit there, knowing that he was about to lose his other leg, and not care?

"Lori," he said, "my childhood was tough, but God made sure that I had people that loved me and took care of me. Life isn't easy, but you need to face it with grace and courage."

That was easier said than done. How could he have so much courage? All my life he's been here for me, and in a few days he may go into the hospital and never come back out.

The days flew by, and before I knew it, the day of the surgery came. Thankfully, he made it through. That night I went to see my dad, and I was shocked by what I saw. Where was the man that I had looked up to all my life? No, the man in that bed was so sick and so old. That was not my dad.

A few days later, I went into my dad's room and asked, "Dad, why don't I have courage and faith like you do?"

"Lori, everyone has courage. You need to believe in yourself, and you'll find that you are stronger than you ever imagined. The courage comes from within you."

The next day my dad died. I walked into the office at school and saw my mom and my aunt there crying. My brother walked in behind me, and I just screamed. We went back home, and I slowly let it sink into my head: My dad was dead. How was I supposed to live without him?

I walked into my parents' room and found my dad's Bible. I paged through it and found a paper with "1 John 5:14-15" written on it. I decided to look it up. It said: "If we ask anything according to his will he hears us. And if we know that he hears us in whatever we ask, we know that we have obtained the requests made of him."

Suddenly I understood what my dad had been trying to tell me all this time: We have to have faith that God will do what is best for us, and courage to face the result.

My dad gave me one of the greatest gifts you can imagine. He gave me the courage to believe in myself and to face life and all its problems. I know that I can do anything I put my mind to, as long as I use the courage that I have within me.

Megan Francis
Bishop Feehan High School
Attleboro, Massachusetts

Who Are the Lucky Ones?

My service project was to go to Wrentham State Hospital to help the residents, mostly elderly, do various projects. The clients were either mentally or physically challenged, and in many cases they were both.

I have a little sister who has special needs, so when I heard that my class was assigned to Wrentham State, I was so excited. I knew what to expect and what to do in most cases with these clients because of my sister, but I was a bit frightened about those who were blind, deaf, or unable to speak.

One of the days we were there made me feel really good. I realized that I was there that day to make one of the women clients, an elderly woman named Mary, happy. Mary was mentally disabled. I will never forget her face when I was introduced to her. She had a big smile, and her eyes brightened with excitement. My group was taking the clients over to the coffeehouse. On the way over, Mary asked me if I was her friend. I told her, "Of course I am." It was obvious that she felt more comfortable, because she held my hand tighter and talked to me more freely.

When we arrived at the coffeehouse, she had so much fun. She danced with practically everyone that night. After I took Mary back to her cottage that night to say good-bye, her last words to me were, "Good-bye, my new friend," with the same smile and bright eyes she'd shown me when we met.

After that I had a definite change in attitude about my own family. I realized how fortunate I am to have a loving mother, father, and two sisters. I also realized how fortunate my sister Colleen is to be with us instead of being in a hospital like Wrentham State. My parents told me that when they were young, most children with problems like Colleen's were placed in hospitals like Wrentham State, and this is most likely what had happened to the people I met there.

Most of the clients that I met at Wrentham State do not have family or friends that visit them. This is really sad to think about, and it is obvious to me that they need more people like us to visit them more frequently. It makes me feel so special to know how much they appreciate my presence each time we visit.

I really enjoyed this project, and I recommend that the Blessed Sacrament confirmation classes continue to do this project for their community service. In fact, I strongly suggest that a larger percentage of classroom time be spent on this project than on classroom work.

At first I felt that I was the lucky one, because I "had more" than the patients at Wrentham State. After much thinking, though, I have come to the conclusion that in a way they are the lucky or blessed ones, and that we have much to learn from them. You see, they have never and will never really know hatred, anger, or bigotry. They are happy with what little they have or receive, and they have only love to give to others in return. I believe that because of this, their path to heaven is already paved. What about us? We're the ones with the greatest job ahead of us: to get to heaven with all those obstacles— hatred, anger, and bigotry—in front of us. After this reflection the question really is, "Who are the *real* lucky ones?"

My Teacher, My Friend

Erin Lopez
Notre Dame High School
San Jose, California

My history teacher and swimming coach, Steve Wishart, is a person who has inspired me to be the best I can be. I heard his first words of encouragement when I joined the swim team.

"Up! Up! Up! Come on, Lopez! Pull harder!" he shouted as I raced. I pulled as hard and as fast as I could. Could I win? As long as I knew my coach believed in me, I knew I could do it.

As I stared at the other end of the pool during my first lap, I heard "Up! Up!" ringing in my ears. My mind was focused, and before I knew it, I was on my nineteenth lap and still hearing his voice in my mind.

Finally, I was on my twentieth lap in the 500-meter free-style. I came up for a breath, and I saw Mr. Wishart walking next to the edge of the pool, shouting at me to go faster. A sudden burst of energy surged through my body, and my legs and arms started to move faster. I touched the wall and looked up. There was Mr. Wishart, extending a helping hand with a smile on his face, even though I had finished fourth. He was proud because I had swum hard and put everything I had into this race. Who knew he would be pleased with fourth place?

But fourth place was not an accepted place for me to be in the classroom. "Are you taking notes, Lopez? Who were the major players in the American Revolution? What was the major reason for the United States to revolt against the British?" he would ask me in class. Yes, I did take notes, and yes, I studied

130

extra hard for tests by typing up my illegible notes so I could read them.

"Good job, Lopez!" Mr. Wishart cheered. "You got an A on this test!" And yes, I ranked higher than fourth place by the end of the year. Actually, I was in the top two percent of United States history students. Mr. Wishart made it possible for me to aim higher, reach my goal, and let my potential show to everyone. He made it possible for me because he gave me the encouragement I needed.

Amazing! Mr. Wishart put all his faith in me, and I fumed my way into becoming one of his best students. Later I became his teacher assistant, helping other students take notes and study for class, making his slide shows, putting grades into the computer, and making tests. I was trusted. It was the greatest feeling a teenager could have, because this is a time in our life when we are not the most trusted people, because of our sometimes difficult transition into adulthood. Mr. Wishart's trust helped me to become a more responsible person. He has helped to mold me into the person I am today.

But Mr. Wishart is not only a teacher, he is also a friend. I go to him for advice about everything—from school to life. Mr. Wishart is a model of what every teacher should be. I now believe that I can be a generous, giving, trustworthy person with a dream. My dream is to be a lab technician doing research. I was inspired to aim high, and I plan to carry this philosophy to college next fall. I found my inspiration in a realistic person who was always there for me, like a friend should be. He is my confidant—the person I talk to the most. He is my inspiration—the person who led me to greatness. That is why Mr. Steve Wishart is my friend, my leader, my inspiration, and my hero.

My Family's Love

Valerie Siow
Saint Catherine
Indian School
Santa Fe, New Mexico

I have found inspiration and hope for the future from my family. Though they may not know it, my mom, dad, and younger sisters have inspired me to reach for the stars. Some motivation also comes from within myself. A fire of passion and excitement burns inside me when I think of my future, because I know that I can be anything I desire to be. I know that I would not feel this way if it were not for my family, because they have put this desire into my heart.

There have been, and still are, times in my life when I would become discouraged and want to give up. When I was younger, I went to an elementary school in Albuquerque where I was one of two Native American students. Many of the other students would not even talk to me; I believed they felt that they were better than me. It was rough for me, and every day I used to dread going to school. My mom knew how I felt, and she taught me to be more sociable and to take a deeper interest in my schoolwork. I learned to be more talkative and less shy. After that, school began to seem more enjoyable, and I had more friends. During that experience my mom was by my side the whole time.

Now I am in my junior year of high school, and the future is starting to seem scary. I have only one more year to go before I move on to college. For a while I was really afraid to even think of college, because I thought that it would be too hard for

132

me, and I might have to drop out. But then I looked at my family. My dad is always tired from work. My mom seems to be stressed out from the pressures of work and family. My younger sisters are lonesome without me because I am away at boarding school. I think of all that my parents have sacrificed through the years to put me through Catholic school, all the time they took off from work to take me places or to attend my volleyball and softball games. Then I think of the kind of world and society that my younger sisters are going to continue to grow up in, and it sometimes depresses me.

I owe it to myself to go to college and make something out of my life. I want to help my parents just as they have helped me. I want them to know that everything they did was well worth it. Most of all, I want to be a role model for my sisters, to show them that it is all right to be into school, and that education is a ticket to anywhere. Neither my mom nor my dad nor anyone else in my family has actually graduated from college, and I would like to be the first to do so. With my example, perhaps more of my family will do the same.

My family is sacred to me. I would not be where I am today without them. The grades I have earned, the honors I have received, and the confidence I have in myself would not have been possible if they had not motivated me to be the best person I can be. I have so many dreams for my future, and because of my family's love, one day my dreams will become a reality.

Index by School

DePaul High School
Wayne, NJ
Angelica Jiménez   102

Divine Child High School
Dearborn, MI
Katie Kalis   96

Father Judge High School
Philadelphia, PA
L. A. A.   22

Incarnate Word High School
San Antonio, TX
Mariel Tatiana Fernandez   42

John F. Kennedy Catholic High School
Warren, OH
Jennifer Green   44

Ladywood High School
Livonia, MI
Kendall Ann Carey   58

Lake Michigan Catholic High School
Saint Joseph, MI
Vicki Miller   56
Maria Steinhauser   120
Katrina Villasis   40

Lancaster Catholic High School
Lancaster, PA
Angela M. Baumler   114

La Salle College High School
Wyndmoor, PA
Joseph D. Crane   50
Matthew Luhks   14

Mercy High School
Omaha, NE
Stacey Larson   cover

Merion Mercy Academy
Merion, PA
K   36
Kathy Cunniffe   66

Mount Carmel Academy
New Orleans, LA
Jennifer Burger   61

Mount Saint Joseph Academy
Flourtown, PA
Rory Murphy   26

Newman Central Catholic High School
Sterling, IL
Mary Hermes   83

Notre Dame High School
San Jose, CA
Erin Lopez   130

Our Lady of Good Council High School
Wheaton, MD
Rebecca Bishop   53

Ramona Convent Secondary School
Alhambra, CA
Pearl Carmen Hernandez   122
Georgina K. Vaca   112

Red Cloud High School
Pine Ridge, SD
Elena Azul Cisneros   12

Sacred Heart School of Montreal
Montreal, Quebec, Canada
M. C.   46

Saint Agnes Academy
Memphis, TN
Brandy Harper   75
Johanna Mihok   101

**Saint Catherine
Indian School**
Santa Fe, NM
Valerie Siow   132

**Saint Catherine's
High School**
Racine, WI
Lori Hennessy   126

Saint Francis School
Honolulu, HI
Sharon Trinidad   88

Saint John's College
Brantford, Ontario, Canada
Alisha Ruiss   106

**Saint Joseph's
Collegiate Institute**
Buffalo, NY
Daniel Barrett   72

Saint Lawrence Academy
Santa Clara, CA
Jennifer Kutsenda   81

Saint Mary's Academy
Nauvoo, IL
Jean Hee Shin   76
Michaela Elizabeth Knipe   90

Saint Mary's Academy
Portland, OR
Emily Bennett   30

Saint Pius X High School
Atlanta, GA
Gerri Sattele   119

Saint Wendelin High School
Fostoria, OH
Jackie Reichert   111

**Saint William of York
Parish**
Baltimore, MD
Name Withheld   116

**Saratoga Central Catholic
High School**
Saratoga Springs, NY
Kate Flanagan   69

Seton Catholic High School
Chandler, AZ
Paul Tomasik   16
Francis A. Zovko   48

Stella Maris High School
Rockaway Park, NY
Shannon Murray   86
Veronika Sweeny   34

Trinity High School
Garfield, OH
Amy Kling   95
Jen Toronski   125